TEACHING COMPUTATIONAL THINKING AND CODING
IN PRIMARY SCHOOLS

Sara Miller McCune founded SAGE Publishing in 1965 to support the dissemination of usable knowledge and educate a global community. SAGE publishes more than 1000 journals and over 800 new books each year, spanning a wide range of subject areas. Our growing selection of library products includes archives, data, case studies and video. SAGE remains majority owned by our founder and after her lifetime will become owned by a charitable trust that secures the company's continued independence.

Los Angeles | London | New Delhi | Singapore | Washington DC | Melbourne

TEACHING COMPUTATIONAL THINKING AND CODING
IN PRIMARY SCHOOLS

DAVID MORRIS,
GURMIT UPPAL and
DAVID WELLS

Learning Matters
An imprint of SAGE Publications Ltd
1 Oliver's Yard
55 City Road
London EC1Y 1SP

SAGE Publications Inc.
2455 Teller Road
Thousand Oaks, California 91320

SAGE Publications India Pvt Ltd
B 1/l 1 Mohan Cooperative Industrial Area
Mathura Road
New Delhi 110 044

SAGE Publications Asia-Pacific Pte Ltd
3 Church Street
#10-04 Samsung Hub
Singapore 049483

Editor: Amy Thornton
Development Editor: Jennifer Clark
Production Controller: Chris Marke
Project Management: Deer Park Productions
Marketing Manager: Dilhara Attygalle
Cover Design: Wendy Scott
Typeset by: C&M Digitals (P) Ltd, Chennai, India
Printed by CPI Group (UK) Ltd, Croydon, CR0 4YY

Library of Congress Control Number: 2017936983

British Library Cataloguing in Publication data

A catalogue record for this book is available from the British Library

ISBN 978-1-4739-8505-6 (pbk)
ISBN 978-1-4739-8504-9

At SAGE we take sustainability seriously. Most of our products are printed in the UK using FSC papers and boards. When we print overseas we ensure sustainable papers are used as measured by the PREPS grading system. We undertake an annual audit to monitor our sustainability.

During the writing of Chapter 3 *Programming with Floor Robots*, Seymour Papert – inventor of the floor and screen turtle and the programming language Logo – sadly passed away. This book is dedicated to the far-reaching impact that his work has had on education and, in particular, on his conviction of children being natural programmers.

Seymour Papert's insights and observations about children, computers, and computer cultures remain timeless.

John Sculley, preface to the 2nd edition of *Mindstorms* 1993.

Seymour Papert
29 February 1928–31 July 2016

Contents

Acknowledgements

The authors would like to thank the following companies and organisations for images reproduced in this book:

2Simple Software

App Inventor

AppShed Ltd.

Dial Solutions Ltd.

DNA Outlet

Flexible Software Ltd.

Gearies Primary School, Redbridge

Kodable

LEGO WeDo

Lightbot

RobotMesh (Flowol)

SAGE (Learning Matters)

Scargill Junior School, Havering

Scratch

Scratch Jr

Swallows Systems

TTS Group Ltd.

Valiant Technology Ltd.

We would like to express our gratitude to Dave Smith and Amanda Jackson (Havering School Improvement Services) for their time, interest and interview for Chapter 6 of this book. The authors would also like to thank Kate Hudson at Valiant for her resourcefulness and wisdom, Emily Barnes for her kind permission to reproduce Figure 2.1 and Sheharbano Ali for her kind permission to use extracts from her 2016 PGCE assignment.

Every effort has been made to contact copyright holders for permission to use the images within this book. In the unlikely event of any omission, this can be rectified in a subsequent edition by contacting the publishers at **https://uk.sagepub.com/en-gb/eur/learning-matters**

About the Authors and Series Editor

Authors

David Morris has had over 20 years' experience in the education sector. Recently retired, David was Senior Lecturer at the Cass School of Education, University of East London where he spent 12 years working in Initial Teacher Education. David has taught in both the primary and secondary sectors and, as a specialist teacher, he has taught ICT and computing to children in every year group from Nursery through to Year 11. David is a published author and has delivered research papers at both national and international conferences.

Gurmit Uppal has 16 years' experience in the education sector. She currently works as a Senior Lecturer at the Cass School of Education, University of East London where she has taught and led computing to trainee teachers for the last six years. Gurmit has also taught in the primary sector for 16 years, where her roles have included subject leadership of ICT and computing. She has worked as a freelance consultant and trainer for an educational e-learning company and is a published author. Her current research interests are in the area of both children's and trainee teachers' understanding of online safety issues.

David Wells is a Senior Lecturer in computing Initial Teacher Education at the Cass School of Education, University of East London. Prior to undertaking this role, David worked for 18 years as a teacher, leader and cross-curricular co-ordinator of Information Technology and computing in secondary schools. David's current research interest focuses on the use of gamification and video game dynamics as a pedagogy to support motivation and engagement in pupils' progress and learning.

Series Editor

Alice Hansen

Alice is the Director of Children Count Ltd, an education consultancy company that provides continuing professional development for teachers in primary mathematics education and primary schools in curriculum development in England and abroad. Prior to her current role, she was a primary school teacher and senior lecturer in primary education before becoming a programme leader of a teacher-training programme. Alice is an active researcher: her interests include primary mathematics, technology-enhanced learning and teacher professional development.

Glossary

In this book you may come across words, phrases and terms that you are unfamiliar with. The following glossary, although not a definitive guide, may be a useful resource to refer to while studying this book.

Abstraction   *Abstraction* manages complexity in problems or systems through the identification of key information and disregarding irrelevant detail.

Academy   A school that is independent of local authority control, but funded directly by the Department for Education.

Action research   An inquiry or area of study conducted by and for the person who wants to take the action, in improving their practice.

AfL (Assessment for learning)   A teaching and learning approach which uses a range of assessment strategies, with the aim of improving pupil performance by involving them actively in learning through effective dialogue and feedback.

Algorithms   Clear and precise step-by-step procedures or rules.

Application (app)   Mobile applications – commonly abbreviated as 'apps' – are software programs which are most commonly created to run on smartphones and tablet devices.

Avatar   An image or character designed to be representative of an individual person on screen and in digital games.

Bloom's taxonomy   A tiered classification that details different learning outcomes and assessment objectives designed to promote higher-order thinking skills in our pupils.

Bluetooth   A wireless technology which allows information to be shared between devices which are in close proximity to each other.

Browser   A software program for retrieving, presenting, and navigating information on the world wide web.

CE   The **Clear Entry** command cancels the previous entry from a floor robot's memory.

CM   The **Clear Memory** command removes all previously stored instructions from a floor robot's memory.

Concept map   A graphical tool used to represent knowledge of a subject and the relationships that exist between aspects of this knowledge.

CP   The **Clear Procedure** command removes a stored procedure from a floor robot's memory.

CPD (Continuing Professional Development) Refers to the activities and training teachers engage with in order to maintain and improve their ability and skillset.

Cross-curricular Teaching and learning episodes which encompass knowledge, skills and understanding from two or more subject areas.

CSS (Cascading Style Sheets) *CSS* contain descriptions of how HTML elements are to be displayed on screen. They can control the layout of multiple web pages all at once and are usually stored in separate *CSS* files.

Decomposition Involves breaking up problems into separate parts which can then be addressed in turn.

Dialogic teaching *Dialogic teaching* (Alexander, 2008) is the effective use of talk between teachers and pupils through using specific strategies.

Differentiation The means by which a planned lesson or activity is made accessible to meet the attainment range within a class or group of children.

Disapply ICT was disapplied as a national curriculum subject, meaning it still had to be taught but individual schools could decide the content and assessment requirements themselves.

Discovery learning A constructivist learning theory based on Jerome Bruner's principles of inquiry-based instruction, and which is closely related to the work of Jean Piaget and Seymour Papert.

DTD: (Document Type Declaration) *DTD* tells the browser the version of HTML a web page is written in.

Ebacc (English Baccalaureate) A performance measure awarded when pupils attain above grade C in a GCSE maths, English, science, languages or humanities programme. It is not a qualification.

Emotional literacy A term used to describe how people are aware of their feelings, understand them and can manage them.

Emulator Emulation software allows users to view and interact with a different device through a simulated computer environment. Emulators are handy when the specified device is not available or no longer operational. Although useful, emulators often have limitations and may not be fully functioning representations of the original device.

Evaluation In computational thinking, *evaluation* is an ongoing methodical action to check the solution meets the requirements of the problem.

Floor robot A generic term used to cover a range of programmable educational toys of different appearance yet similar function.

Flow chart   A diagram which provides a visual representation of an algorithm. It uses specific symbols for decisions, steps and processes.

For loop   A for loop (or loop) is an instruction given to a computer to carry out a task a specified amount of times. Most loops work by using a variable as a counter. In Logo, the letter i is the name of the counter variable, and three numbers are used to indicate where the counter begins, ends and what the step should be. In Scratch, blocks with 'forever' or 'repeat' are both loop constructs.

Free school   A school set up to be funded by the state as a non-profit making organisation, not under the control of local authorities.

FSM (Free School Meal)   Pupils eligible for **FSM** are often used as a benchmark for analysing outcomes of those considered to be disadvantaged financially.

Gamification   A pedagogy that utilises game dynamics, mechanics and aesthetics in delivering lessons and learning – see Chapter 8 for more details.

GaT   Pupils identified by the school to be **Gifted and Talented** in a specific area of the curriculum/wider curriculum.

GCSE (General Certificate of Secondary Education)   The qualifications taken at the end of the Key Stage 4 curriculum.

GIGO (Garbage in Garbage Out)   A computer will invalidate any instruction it has not been programmed to do and will produce an error message.

HTML (Hyper Text Mark-up Language)   Used to encode web pages which can contain URLs that reference other web pages elsewhere.

HTTP (Hyper Text Transfer Protocol)   A language understood by both web clients (such as Safari, Chrome, Firefox) and servers.

Hyperlink   A link from a hypertext document to another location, activated by clicking on a highlighted word or image.

Hypertext   A non-sequential text that can follow links to other sources of information.

Input   Data or information which is received by a computerised system.

Internet   A vast communications infrastructure which connects computers together allowing them to communicate with each other.

Intrinsic motivation   The motivation comes from within the person, arising from internal rather than external rewards.

JavaScript   A dynamic computer programming language commonly used alongside HTML.

LAC   Refers to **Looked After Children** and children in care.

Logical reasoning   Required throughout all computational thinking processes to predict, analyse and check information.

Logo   A list-processing language invented by Seymour Papert and Marvin Minskey at the Massachusetts Institute of Technology (MIT) in 1967–68. As a programming language, Logo uses three kinds of data: numbers, words and lists.

Markup   A process which originates from the traditional editorial process where paper manuscripts were annotated with written instructions for revisions.

National Curriculum (NC)   Sets out the programmes of study for all subjects at all four key stages.

Non-verbal reasoning   A cognitive process which involves the ability to understand and analyse information and solve problems using visual reasoning.

Notepad   A basic text editor for creating simple documents and often used to create code for web pages.

Output   Data or information which is sent from a computerised system.

PA   Refers to those pupils who are **Persistently Absent**.

Paired programming   A collaborative approach to programming where two individuals work at the same computer taking turns to input and review the code.

Pattern recognition or generalisation   The identification of patterns is an efficient approach which allows computer scientists to identify generalisations and lead to a solution or model which can be reused.

Pedagogy   The theory and thinking behind the practice of teaching, how best to teach and how best to get your pupils learning.

Peer assessment   A well-documented formative assessment method whereby pupils review and mark each other's work with a view to improving their subsequent work and learning. Peer assessment is argued to improve a pupil's diagnostic and evaluative capability.

Personalisation   The means by which learning is planned in direct response to the individual who is encouraged to drive and take ownership of the learning.

Pixel   The smallest element on a computer display screen.

Platform   The software or hardware environment of tablets, smartphones and laptops. Apple and Android are the most commonly known platforms for mobile devices, although several other platforms exist including Windows and BlackBerry.

Primitive   An individual command which constitutes the simplest element available in a programming language.

Procedure A defined and stored set of instructions.

Programme of Study (PoS) A subject syllabus that must be followed for all key stages of the national curriculum.

Programming The result of an algorithm being expressed using a specific form or code which can be understood by a computer.

Pseudo code A way of describing a set of instructions required in the program being developed. It is a way of representing the algorithm without using the specific syntax of the programming tool.

Pupil premium Additional funding for state schools in England designed to support investment in raising the achievement of disadvantaged pupils.

Questioning Effective *questioning* is one of the most powerful formative assessment tools a teacher can use in checking their pupils' understanding. It will often be structured as open or closed approaches that are linked to Bloom's taxonomy.

RAG A way of allocating a colour (**Red/Amber/Green**) to identify pupil progress. Red signifies not making progress; Amber equates to being on target; and Green suggests working above expected levels.

RGB Stands for **Red Green Blue** (a standard colour model in computing).

SATs (Standard Assessment Tests) Taken by pupils in England as part of their national curriculum study, at the end of Key Stages 1, 2 and 3.

Scaffolding A step-by-step process where supporting strategies and structures are put in place during the initial stages of learning new concepts, and later removed as expertise develops.

Script A script in programming is a sequence of instructions which, when executed, are interpreted one-by-one.

SDLC (Systems {software} Development Life Cycle) A project management concept that describes the stages/phases involved in developing or building an information system. There are various models and methodologies that can be used to define, plan, develop, implement and maintain such systems.

Self-assessment Pupils mark and assess their own work allowing them to deepen their knowledge of what they are learning and the outcomes expected.

SEND Pupils identified as having *Special Educational Needs or Disabilities*.

Set Pupils are placed in ability-based classes in a particular subject.

Simulation A computer *simulation* is a model or application of a real-life situation.

Source code The 'markup' code of any web page.

SoW (scheme of work) A document which outlines the teaching of a subject or curriculum area across year groups or age phases.

Sprite A graphic which can programmed. For example, in Scratch, the cat character is the default sprite.

Stream Pupils are placed in classes based on their ability. They stay in these classes for all subjects.

Syntax Refers to the words used, as well as the spelling and grammatical requirements of a programming language.

Tab A feature of a web browser that enables you to open multiple web pages in a single window.

Tag A code that describes how a particular element of a web page is formatted.

URLs (Uniform Resource Locators) Unique identifiers for each and every web page.

Variable Any data where the value is not constant or fixed and can be changed, e.g. colour, size.

Waterfall method The oldest of all SDLC methodologies. The output of one stage becomes the input of the next stage e.g. the output of the investigation stage becomes the input to the analysis.

WWW (world wide web) The medium or way in which information is accessed over the internet.

1 An Introduction to the Computing Curriculum

Learning outcomes

By the end of this chapter you will have:

- developed an introductory understanding of the computing curriculum;
- considered the Information and Communications Technology (ICT) to computing curriculum shift.

Teachers' Standards

A teacher must:

3. Demonstrate good subject and curriculum knowledge:

- demonstrate a critical understanding of developments in the subject and curriculum areas, and promote the value of scholarship.

Part Two. Personal and professional conduct:

- teachers must have an understanding of, and always act within, the statutory frameworks which set out their professional duties and responsibilities.

(DfE, 2011)

Introduction

This chapter will introduce you to computing in the English primary phase curriculum. It will summarise the historical input of Information Technology (IT) and Information and Communications Technology (ICT), and position computing as a highly important subject in any school's academic provision. The book you are now beginning to read will offer guidance, support, ideas and tools for implementing, delivering and assessing a successful computing curriculum at Key Stages 1 and 2. Although the computing programmes of study (PoS) are non-statutory in the Early Years Foundation Stage (EYFS), guidance is given to those teaching this age phase.

September 2014 saw the introduction of the 'new' national curriculum in England, including computing (DfE, 2013a). Not all schools, however, are obliged to follow the programmes of study as detailed in this national curriculum. Independent schools, academies and free schools are exempt, although they are expected to provide a *broad and balanced* curriculum for their pupils. Academies and free schools, for example, must offer English, maths, science, religious education and sex and relationships education. If they have Reception and pre-school pupils, then the *Statutory Framework for the Early Years Foundation stage* is to be followed (DfE, 2014). All national tests such as Key Stage 2 Standard Attainment Tests (SATs) must also be adhered to. In practice, most of these schools deliver the majority of the national curriculum subjects as set out in the 2014 documentation.

Computing is a new compulsory subject in this latest national curriculum iteration, taught at all phases from Key Stage 1 to Key Stage 4 (ages 5 through to 16). Previously Information and Communications Technology (ICT) was taught in UK primary and secondary schools. This ICT curriculum had been under considerable review prior to 2014, with many industry leaders and academics calling for change. September 2012 saw the ICT programmes of study, attainment targets and associated statutory assessment expectations 'disapplied' from the then national curriculum. This removed a programme and subject that the Secretary of State for Education at the time described as *too off-putting, too de-motivating, too dull* (Gove, 2012). ICT still had to be studied in our schools but teachers were given the freedom to decide their own taught content and not be tied to the national curriculum programme. Computing and computer science are, at the time of writing, the options perceived as the route forward for appropriate academic and vocational engagement in the subject area (DfE, 2015).

What is computing?

The computing curriculum has been 'disaggregated' into three clearly defined areas (Morris, 2012) and as a discipline, is made up of the following subject strands: Digital Literacy, Information Technology and computer science (Royal Society, 2012). Digital literacy can be referred to as the knowledge, competence and skills needed to access and use a range of technological devices. Information Technology is the use of computer systems to create, store, process, manipulate and share digital information and data. computer science is the study of the theory behind the technology we now use. It is concerned with how computers, digital equipment and their software work, are implemented, and are designed. It involves the science of programming and computational thinking and as such goes beyond the comparatively simple use and exchange of electronic information that IT and Digital Literacy facilitate. This 'shift' represents considerable challenge for many primary teachers, and it is hoped this book will help alleviate some of this challenge for you entering the profession, and demystify computer science as a perceived (too) complex subject to engage with. The purpose of this book is not, therefore, to discuss the Digital Literacy and IT elements of the computing curriculum. Instead, the following chapters will focus on the teaching of computer science and its computational thinking foundations.

A brief history of IT, ICT and CS in our schools

Information Technology and ICT had been an established national curriculum subject for over 20 years, before the introduction and transference to computing took place. The final version of the ICT national curriculum programme of study (PoS), published in 2007, detailed the following skills and processes as required to be learned:

- *Finding Information* – concerned with solving problems and the ability to collect and search for data and information while judging its value, accuracy, validity, reliability and bias;

- *Developing Ideas* – creating models and IT systems that make things happen by planning, testing and modifying a sequence of instructions, recognising where a group of instructions needs repeating, and automating frequently-used processes by constructing efficient procedures that are fit for purpose;

- *Communicating Information* – presenting, exchanging and communicating information safely and responsibly;

- *Evaluating* – reflecting critically by reviewing, modifying and evaluating work as it is being completed.

(The Qualifications and Curriculum Authority, 2007)

An interesting observation when considering this 'old' ICT programme of study, is that it should dispel any myths you might have that ICT was simply about using application software such as word processing and desktop publishing. This is how the curriculum was often *interpreted* by schools. With this in mind, recent ICT education had arguably focused on the *training of office skills* (Livingstone and Hope, 2011). However, this was not what the curriculum was designed to do in progressing our pupils' IT competence and capability.

It can therefore be contended that the previous ICT curriculum was not working for a*ll* pupils in maintaining the challenge and progress needed for the twenty-first century (Wells, 2012). Vocational ICT qualifications (in particular) achieved significant outcomes and success at the end of Key Stage 4 for countless pupils. However, many schools were interpreting their ICT curriculum from its lowest level of need (Royal Society, 2012), and using non-specialist teachers to deliver it, meaning appropriate challenge and engagement was not always experienced by our pupils. 'A' Level and undergraduate take-up of computer science courses had also declined dramatically in recent years, indicating difficulty in the UK's ability to sustain its rich heritage as leaders and innovators in the fields of technology and computing. With all this in mind, it would seem relevant and appropriate, therefore, that computing has been introduced as a replacement for what ICT had become in many schools: both to reinvigorate the challenge and rationale of studying within the field (particularly in our more able pupils perhaps) and to meet the growing needs of industry. Clearly, this has more significant implications for secondary school teachers of computing. However, if we are to produce the next generation of programmers and game designers (for example), and encourage a greater take-up of the subject at this level, then there is a clear sense to starting this process with very young children during their primary phase education. It is also worth noting that the science of computational thinking is an excellent cross-curricular and life 'skill' for pupils to engage with, as you will hopefully see as you delve further into this book.

The 'new' and transformed (2014) computing curriculum aims to ensure all pupils:

- can understand and apply the fundamental principles and concepts of computer science, including abstraction, logic, algorithms and data representation;
- can analyse problems in computational terms, and have repeated practical experience of writing computer programs in order to solve such problems;
- can evaluate and apply information technology, including new or unfamiliar technologies, analytically to solve problems;
- are responsible, competent, confident and creative users of information and communication technology.

(DfE, 2013a)

This is broken down into distinct learning expectations and outcomes for each key stage (that will be explored further in subsequent chapters of this book). Computing, although incorporating elements of ICT in its Digital Literacy and IT strands, is therefore a very different subject to what ICT was often interpreted as in schools. Computer science is a more complex area of study than ICT, and as such needs time and effort in developing the skillset to teach these lessons successfully and effectively. The traditional curriculum model of teaching pupils to be *users* of technology is now at conflict with the need for improved subject and pedagogical knowledge required to teach our children to become *creators* of computing innovations (Goode *et al.,* 2012). However, this is not something you should fear and we hope this book will help you to see the relevance of the subject and also that it need not be as complicated as you might think! computer science is not this mythical, complex beast many believe it to be – at least it need not be in Key Stages 1 and 2.

Research focus: shut down or restart

The way forward for computing in UK schools?

Launched in January 2012, this report, by the British Computing Society (published by The Royal Society), details the arguments for either *shutting* ICT down as a curriculum subject, or *rebooting* it as something different and arguably more relevant for our pupils and the UK economy. The report suggested the terminology reform from ICT to the more distinctive three strands of Digital Literacy, IT and computer science. It also makes further recommendations for how to overhaul the ICT curriculum and why this change was needed. As a starting point for considering the curriculum shift that has been taking place since September 2012, it is highly recommended that you engage with this influential report.

Activity: reflection point

In your opinion:

Where do you position yourself in this curriculum shift from ICT to computing? Was it necessary? Can primary school colleagues meet the demands of the new curriculum for computing? Will schools engage with the computer science strand of the curriculum or err on Digital Literacy and IT?

The need for pedagogic shift and change?

The introduction of computer science as a discipline within computing has caused considerable issues and anxieties for many teachers. Inevitably change often breeds fear and reluctance in people to embrace that change. They are concerned about being able to successfully make the transition from the familiar (ICT) to the new (computer science). They are concerned about the impact on their role and inevitable employment. They struggle to see the arguments and reasons presented for the change because the change is unfamiliar to them. However, the change has happened, and schools and colleagues teaching in them are in a position where they must implement change. With reference to Kurt Lewin's 1951 change management model, teachers must *unfreeze* and, with the appropriate *driving forces* (which this book will hopefully contribute to), teachers will be able to transition successfully and confidently into this 'unknown'.

As a beginning primary teacher, you are in a position to act as an 'agent of change' (and therefore a driving force) in supporting this successful transition in your training schools.

The expertise to deliver computing-focused lessons may not exist with many of your primary school colleagues and this will inevitably impact on the school's ability to provide creative and imaginative computer science lessons. You can help support this and bridge computing 'capability gaps' by sharing your own knowledge and expertise, as well as suggesting pedagogy that might be used for successful learning within computing to support the required 'pedagogic shift' within this subject.

Research focus: change agents

Stevenson (2008) suggests that a change agent is about identity, understanding people, being self-motivational, patient and living for the future. To complement this, Lu and Ortlieb (2009) suggest change agents are innovators, initiators, creators, convincers and involvers. An agent of change will have a *vision* that they see as possible to enact. They will be somebody who is empowered to influence others in both purpose and focus (Price and Valli, 2005). Change agents will want to make a difference and are able to inspire transformation (Dunne and Zandstra, 2011). They are originators and designers of new initiatives and strategies (Healey, 2014) that change the educational backdrop they inhabit.

Teachers' anxieties and fears have often centred on their lack of content understanding, and efforts to support change to computing are frequently focused on the subject matter of the new curriculum (Goode *et al.*, 2012). Whereas this is important in developing the confidence to teach computing at all key stages, so is the *pedagogical shift* needed to successfully enable appropriate learning with what the new curriculum is asking for. The way ICT has traditionally been taught in our schools is not necessarily how computer science should be taught. The pedagogy of skills training in specific programming packages, for example, is unlikely to inspire our pupils to wish to enthusiastically engage with new computing subject content. A more pupil-centred, creative, innovative, problem-solving, error-making, exploratory and experimental approach may be more fitting. Simply demonstrating Scratch skills (as an example) that pupils then replicate in their work to become Scratch 'experts' is not enough. This is not enough to develop the confidence in developing and engaging pupils in their understanding and application of programming concepts and computational thinking.

Therefore, transforming teacher pedagogy within computing is of huge worth. Simply handing teachers a new curriculum (Goode *et al.*, 2012) and providing content training is not satisfactory. Teachers at the start of their career (i.e. *you*) acting as collaborative agents of change (with support from their teacher education programmes and this book) can begin to enable this required change and development – both in knowledge gain and pedagogical expertise. Do not be under any misapprehensions though. It will take you time and considerable commitment to develop the subject knowledge and pedagogical approaches to successfully begin to meet and create the change needed. This book is written to support this development.

Activity: reflection point

So what do you think? What do your colleagues on your course and in your schools think? Do we need to rethink how we teach computing (and particularly computer science)? Is this important? Why?

What can you offer your schools in developing subject knowledge and pedagogy within computing? What do you need to do to fulfil this offer?

To conclude

Computing needs to be fun, enjoyable, exciting, creative, innovative, investigative and probing. It needs to allow for errors and mistakes and the development of the resilience and self-efficacy needed to create solutions. It needs conceptual understanding and not just the application and training of skillsets. It doesn't always need computers. 'Unplugged' computing lessons, where computers and digital technology are not used, can be highly effective. The success of primary phase computing rests with you and your peers. You are the ones who will develop this success and create transformational change within your schools regarding computing learning and teaching. The chapters of this book will take you on the journey needed to confidently support this happening. We have aimed to make the chapter content interesting and useful in developing your capability to deliver the computer science strand of the computing national curriculum, with self-assurance and impact. We wish you the best of luck as you begin this challenging, but highly important journey with your pupils.

Learning outcomes review

This chapter has aimed to introduce computing as a new and significant subject within a school's curriculum with the intention of developing your self-assurance and the impact you can have. There are many reasons argued in the literature (e.g. Royal Society, 2012) for why ICT was required to shift to something more relevant and perhaps more challenging for our pupils. Computing is the 'new' curriculum, and forms the current

(Continued)

(Continued)

programme of study for most schools to follow. It is a compulsory subject, meaning it needs to be covered in all key stages from 1 to 4. Primary schools should be making provision within computing, for all pupils in Key Stages 1 and 2. With this in mind, let us reflect on the learning outcomes for this chapter:

- **Developed an introductory understanding of the computing curriculum;**
  How are your placement schools embedding computing in their curriculums?
  Is it actually computing they are developing and teaching or ICT?
  What content is being covered? How? When? Where? How often do lessons take place?
  What support are you able to offer in helping the schools develop a computing-focused curriculum?

- **Considered the Information and Communications Technology (ICT) to computing curriculum shift.**
  How well positioned in this 'shift' do you see yourself and your placement schools?
  Do your placement schools understand what this shift represents in terms of content to be learned?
  Does the maths and literacy focus mean that other subject areas are being squeezed in terms of time on the curriculum? What impact might this be having on computing learning and achievement?

Further reading and resources

Berry, M (2013b) *Computing in the National Curriculum: A guide for primary teachers.* CAS. London. Available at: **www.computingatschool.org.uk/data/uploads/CASPrimary Computing.pdf** (accessed 17 February 2017).

A starting point in planning your primary computing curriculum lessons.

Computing at School (CAS) Working Group (2012) *Computer science: a curriculum for schools.* CAS. London. Available at: **https://www.computingatschool.org.uk/data/uploads/ ComputingCurric.pdf** (accessed 17 February 2017).

A useful starting point in determining what might form a computer science-focused curriculum.

Department for Education (DfE) (2013) *National curriculum in England: computing programmes of study.* Available at: **www.gov.uk/government/publications/**

national-curriculum-in-england-computing-programmes-of-study/national-curriculum-in-england-computing-programmes-of-study (accessed 17 February 2017).

The current computing national curriculum guidance in its entirety, as published September 2013.

Royal Society (2012) *Shut down or restart? A way forward for computing in UK schools.* The Royal Society. London. Available at: **https://royalsociety.org/~/media/education/computing-in-schools/2012-01-12-computing-in-schools.pdf** (accessed 17 February 2017).

A highly significant report that sets out the case for computing change.

2 Developing Computational Thinking in the Early Years Foundation Stage (EYFS), KS1 and KS2

Learning outcomes

By the end of this chapter you should be able to:

- identify computational thinking as an essential skill which goes beyond the requirements of the computing curriculum;
- recognise the key processes and approaches involved in computational thinking;
- be familiar with approaches to computational thinking in the EYFS, KS1 and KS2;
- identify ideas to incorporate unplugged activities into your lessons to develop computational thinking.

Teachers' Standards

A teacher must:

2. Promote good progress and outcomes by pupils:

- be aware of pupils' capabilities and their prior knowledge, and plan teaching to build on these.

3. Demonstrate good subject and curriculum knowledge:

- have a secure knowledge of the relevant subject(s) and curriculum areas, foster and maintain pupils' interest in the subject, and address misunderstandings;
- demonstrate a critical understanding of developments in the subject and curriculum areas, and promote the value of scholarship.

4. Plan and teach well-structured lessons:

- promote a love of learning and children's intellectual curiosity;
- contribute to the design and provision of an engaging curriculum within the relevant subject area(s).

(DfE, 2011)

Introduction

Computational thinking is a fundamental skill for everyone, not just for computer scientists. To reading, writing and arithmetic, we should add computational thinking to every child's analytical ability (Wing, 2006). The term computational thinking was first introduced by Seymour Papert (1980) and more recently rejuvenated by Jeanette Wing (2006). Despite its name, the potential of computational thinking in developing children's approaches to thinking and learning has always aspired to move beyond its obvious connections to technology. Computational thinking should not be seen as a skill which can exclusively be executed by experienced computer scientists working in complex technological environments; instead it should be seen as an efficient approach to problem solving which can be applied in any area of the curriculum or everyday life. Computational thinking now provides the bedrock for an ambitious computing curriculum which informs schools of their duty to *equip pupils to use computational thinking and creativity to understand and change the world* (DfE, 2013a). While programming and coding have certainly become the buzz words to emerge from the revised computing curriculum, it is important to remember that developing children's thinking skills and capacity for problem solving (Davies, 2014) should be seen as some of the greatest and most transferable benefits of teaching computing in schools.

What is computational thinking?

Computational thinking encompasses the processes, approaches and steps which we deploy to tackle problems and formulate solutions which can *be carried out by a human or machine, or more generally, by combinations of humans and machines* (Wing, 2011). It should be remembered that computational thinking and programming are not the same, and while some form of programming may be required to explain or execute the solution to a problem, computational thinking does not need to culminate in programming or take place at a computer (and therefore 'unplugged'). Instead, the focus should be on the thought processes used.

Although there is no commonly accepted set of skills which define computational thinking (Barr *et al.*, 2011), some processes frequently deployed during computational thinking may include:

- **Logical reasoning**

  Logical reasoning is required throughout all computational thinking processes in allowing pupils to build on their existing knowledge to predict, analyse and check information.

- **Decomposition**

  Decomposition involves breaking up problems into separate parts which can then be addressed in turn. For example, creating a packed lunch could be broken down into the separate tasks of making a sandwich, creating a fruit salad and selecting a drink.

- **Abstraction**

  Abstraction manages complexity in problems or systems through the identification of key information over irrelevant detail. Maps provide a good example of abstraction, where key information is provided, but additional detail may be absent. For example, the London Underground map shows stations, lines and interchanges but distances and geographical locations are not included.

- **Pattern recognition or generalisation**

  The identification of patterns and the ability to make generalisations assists in encouraging pupils to use efficient approaches. The ability to apply and transfer knowledge and skills from one context to another is a higher-order skill which can be developed by encouraging pupils to identify similarities, repeated instructions and make adaptations of existing solutions.

- **Algorithms**

  Algorithms are clear and precise step-by-step procedures or rules. Algorithms are present in every aspect of school life: the managing of class lines in the playground; guiding a child on how to tie her shoe laces; and modelling how to carry out long division in a mathematics lesson. Creating, correcting and refining algorithms requires perseverance, but is an imperative skill for pupils to develop as they learn to build their own programs.

- **Evaluation**

  Evaluation in computational thinking should be viewed as an ongoing action to check the solution meets the requirements of the problem. Evaluation should be a methodical process which is clearly based on the requirements and criteria of the given problem. In classrooms, peer and self-assessment can be utilised for evaluative activities.

(Adapted from Berry, 2015 and Csizmadia et al., 2015)

In addition to the processes of computational thinking, there are different approaches which may be deployed when tackling problems. These include: tinkering (experimenting and playing), creating solutions, debugging (finding and fixing errors), perseverance and collaboration (CAS Barefoot Computing, 2014).

Computational thinking can be developed across many different curriculum areas and this will be be discussed later in Chapter 9. As well as cross-curricular ideas, the use of everyday examples can be hugely beneficial in introducing and understanding computational thinking processes. Computational thinking can be demystified when we consider how we deploy such approaches in typical everyday processes. For example, let us look at the process of making toast.

Table 2.1 Making toast (start and end states)

Start state	End state
Closed sliced loaf of bread	Closed reduced sliced loaf of bread
Untoasted bread	Toasted bread
Toaster off and cold	Toaster off and warm
Butter/spread tub closed	Butter/spread tub closed but reduced
Clean knife	Used knife
Empty plate	Plate containing toast

To move from the start to the end state will involve several computational thinking processes. First, the decision to make toast requires logical reasoning, including prediction when deciding quantities. We demonstrate decomposition in breaking the process into smaller steps and follow an algorithm to reach the end state. Along the way, the algorithm may require adaptation or debugging if the toast gets burnt, is undercooked, or quantities change. Pattern recognition may be called upon if making several rounds of toast, abstraction will be required to ignore the functions of the toaster which are not required, and of course evaluative judgements will be made along the way. As well as the computational thought processes in use, the example outlined above can also introduce discussion around inputs, outputs, loops and variables. Turning everyday activities into processes and algorithms can be a highly useful approach in providing context and tangibility to abstract ideas at any stage of schooling.

Activity: computational thinking in everyday life

The thought processes deployed in computational thinking are similar to those we use in everyday decisions and problems we solve. Think of an everyday activity which you complete, for example, a daily commute on public transport, making a sandwich or washing your hair. Draw or list the steps which need to be carried out to complete the activity from start to finish.

(Continued)

(Continued)

1. Which of the processes listed below did you use and how?
2. Having created an algorithm for your activity, consider how your information is best presented. You may wish to try creating a flowchart, branching database or using image or language-based code.

- Logical reasoning
- Decomposition
- Abstraction
- Pattern recognition
- Algorithms
- Evaluation

The development of computational thinking through the key stages

The development and progression of children's computational thinking links well to psychologist Jerome Bruner's (1960) three stages or modes of cognitive representation: the enactive mode, the iconic mode and the symbolic mode. In Bruner's model, the enactive mode (or concrete stage) involves physical, tangible actions as the first stage of learning. This is then followed by the iconic (or pictoral) mode which uses images and visuals to represent the concrete stage. The final stage of the model is the symbolic (or abstract) mode which builds on the images of the pictoral stage by introducing words and symbols to explain concepts. The use of such a concrete, pictoral to abstract (CPA) approach can and should be applied in all key stages. In the following case study, you can see how Susan uses such a concrete, pictoral to abstract approach in an EYFS Reception class.

Case study: concrete, pictoral to abstract

Susan was completing her final primary PGCE placement in a Reception class in a large three form entry school. As part of the training expectations for the final placement, Susan was expected to take over the full roles and responsibilities of her classroom mentor, which included planning for both continuous and enhanced provision within the setting. Having recently adopted a mathematics mastery approach in KS1 and 2, the concrete, pictoral and abstract approach was encouraged as a key teaching strategy across the school.

Based around the topic of food, Susan set up a restaurant role-play area where pupils could interact with small world toys and play equipment to create meals and serve customers.

→

The restaurant kitchen area included picture cards for pupils to sequence recipe stages for making various food and drink items. In the 'front of house' area, pupils were trained as waiters to welcome guests, take orders, serve and take payment. Once the restaurant role-play area was established, Susan deployed additional adults to adopt the role of new waiters and cooks to observe and question pupils' understanding of instructions and sequencing in line with the Early Learning Goal, *to follow instructions involving several ideas or actions. They answer 'how' and 'why' questions about their experiences and in response to stories or events* (DfE, 2014:10).

Despite making no use of actual technology within the restaurant role-play area, the space did provide a foundation for pupils' computational thinking. Pupils were able to gain concrete, hands-on experience of preparing food and drinks. They were exposed to visual (pictoral) resources to show their ability to correctly sequence recipes. Through discussion, waiters and cooks were able to use language (abstract) to communicate and explain their ideas and instructions. During feedback with her visiting tutor, Susan was able to identify how her role-play area allowed pupils to develop several computational thinking skills, which included decomposition to break down tasks; the use of algorithms in providing and following instructions, and developing abstraction skills when required to summarise and prioritise instructions.

Computational thinking in the EYFS

Although computational thinking is not mentioned in the EYFS Framework, teaching children how to think about thinking can and should begin at an early age. Research by Mittermeir (2013) concluded that children of pre-school age were capable of designing, explaining and understanding algorithms (as step-by-step procedures) if introduced in an age-appropriate manner. With this in mind, a closer look at the EYFS Statutory Framework outlines a key criterion of effective teaching and learning as, *creating and thinking critically {where} children have and develop their own ideas, make links between ideas, and develop strategies for doing things* (DfE, 2014:9). The non-statutory EYFS guidance outlined in Development Matters (The British Association for Early Childhood Education (BAECE), 2012), goes further in providing ideas for several potential areas where young children can be engaging in the development of computational thinking skills, including:

- the following of instructions involving several ideas and actions;
- answering 'how' and 'why' questions;
- encouraging children to describe and solve problems;
- learning through trial and error;
- making predictions;
- orderings numbers;
- recognising, creating and describe patterns;
- representing ideas in various forms.

Activity: planning for computational thinking in the EYFS

As part of a topic based on 'Detectives' a crime scene investigation area has been created in the Early Years environment.

- Consider how this topic and role-play area can be linked to the development of computational thinking processes, such as decomposition, abstraction and pattern recognition.
- Based on this topic, are there any opportunities for pupils to create, follow, debug or explain algorithms?
- In addition to computational thinking, explore opportunities for pupils to *select and use technology for specific purposes* (DfE, 2014:12) within the role-play area.

Figure 2.1 EYFS role-play area

Computational thinking in Key Stage 1

The computer science-related content of the Key Stage 1 computing curriculum (DfE, 2013a), requires pupils to:

- understand what algorithms are, how they are implemented as programs on digital devices, and that programs execute by following precise and unambiguous instructions;

- create and debug simple programs;
- use logical reasoning to predict the behaviour of simple programs.

Various approaches can be taken to achieve these objectives in the classroom, and while all three objectives mention 'programs' this should not automatically be viewed as code-based programming languages such as those used in Scratch, Logo or Kodu. In recent years, primary schools have adopted the use of various programming tools and applications for programming. The benefits and appeal of such resources will be discussed elsewhere in this book, but it should be noted that, without careful planning for progression of computational thinking skills, the use of such tools could lead to gaps and missed opportunities for pupils during the important planning stages which need to take place before programming.

Figures 2.2 and 2.3 are taken from a 2Simple 2Code (Purple Mash by 2Simple - © 2Simple Limited, 2016), Year 2 activity based around air traffic control. Like other similar subscription-based products, 2Code activities provide a series of lesson plans and online activities which guide pupils through creating simple programs using a drag and drop interface, as well as offering debugging challenges and free code programming. The in-built support, rewards, lesson plans, clear curriculum coverage and progression have a great deal to offer schools that may be looking for an 'off the shelf' solution for computing. Teachers are encouraged to further develop such content by ensuring delivery is clearly situated within a computational thinking framework. For example, the activity outlined in Figures 2.2 and 2.3 can be extended through questioning which encourages pupils to share their thought processes:

- Why doesn't the algorithm work?
- What have you already tried?
- Which steps/commands are needed for the yellow plane to take off from the runway?
- There are too many aeroplanes taking off at the same time. Why is this an issue? How can it be avoided?
- Can you explain/write/draw your algorithm for me?
- Are there any parts of your program which are the same?
- How could your airport program be improved?

As pupils progress from one key stage to the next, computational thinking should also encourage pupils to develop autonomy in their approach to problem solving and to combat any *learnt helplessness* (Bagge, 2015) which pupils may have picked up along the way. Phil Bagge (2015) describes learnt helplessness as situations where pupils may expect others to find solutions when obstacles are encountered. Learnt helplessness may display

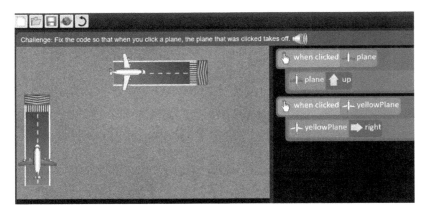

Figure 2.2 2Simple 2Code Debugging activity

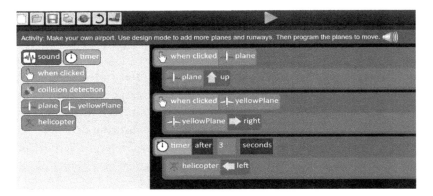

Figure 2.3 2Simple 2Code Free code activity

Images from *Purple Mash* by 2Simple - © 2Simple Limited

itself in many forms in the classroom, from sweet to aggressive demands or complaints about tasks, but it is something which teachers will need to combat and discourage if they are to ensure that pupils are meeting the requirements of the curriculum.

From KS1, the computing curriculum requires children to create and debug *their own* programs as well as using logical reasoning (DfE, 2013a), therefore such opportunities must be provided to pupils, and be viewed as learning opportunities. The role of teachers and additional adults will, therefore, require a shift away from being the problem-solver for the children, towards encouraging children to use strategies which enable them to overcome barriers and make discoveries for themselves. This kind of pupil-centred approach is by no means new or unique to the computing curriculum. It is something which all teachers aspire to, but can easily be forgotten in the midst of busy, demanding and results-driven classroom environments.

Computational thinking in Key Stage 2

The computer science-related content of the KS2 computing curriculum (DfE, 2013a), requires pupils to:

- design, write and debug programs that accomplish specific goals, including controlling or simulating physical systems; solve problems by decomposing them into smaller parts;
- use sequence, selection, and repetition in programs; work with variables and various forms of input and output;
- use logical reasoning to explain how some simple algorithms work and to detect and correct errors in algorithms and programs;
- understand computer networks, including the internet; how they can provide multiple services, such as the world wide web, and the opportunities they offer for communication and collaboration.

As pupils move into KS2, the sophistication and detail of their algorithms, debugging and ability to tackle problems will further develop. As their problem solving becomes more complex, decomposition becomes a requirement to break the problem into smaller steps. More multi-layered programming requires greater efficiency through repetition, loops and sequencing – and pupils are introduced to the wider range of options to adapt their programs through various inputs, outputs and variables. For pupils to create a computer model simulation or program of a real-life scenario they will first need a clear visualised plan for the workings of the system. For these fundamentals of the planning process to be in place before programming can take place, teachers should not be afraid of moving away from the computer and going back to concrete and pictoral approaches to ensure pupils have secure understanding of the problem, its components and explore possible solutions before computer-based programming begins.

The use of flowcharts can be useful in providing visual, step-by-step representations of algorithms. One example of flowchart software is Flowol (Robot Mesh, 2016) software. It allows pupils to create flowchart-based algorithms to control a simulated real-world situation. The Flowal screenshot (Figure 2.4) depicts a pre-loaded mimic of a traffic light simulation, which requires two sets of traffic lights to be correctly programmed to avoid collisions. Problem solving in this activity can start with ensuring children understand the sequence of traffic lights – something which even experienced road users can struggle with when having to recall the sequence away from the road. Pupils would benefit from seeing traffic lights in action, either in the school locality or perhaps on video, before moving on to providing a visual- or language-based representation of the light sequence. Flowcharts – either produced using software such as Flowol or as paper-based diagrams – allow pupils to visualise programming, using specific shapes for different types of actions, deciding on which inputs and outs should be on or off, as well as joining arrows to show sequencing and loops. For teachers, flowcharts can be a useful assessment tool in providing a clear representation of pupils' logical approach to the problem, as well as their ability to create and correctly sequence algorithms based around specific decisions and conditions.

The advantage of using software, such as Flowol, over paper-based diagrams is that the software allows pupils to run their program to check if it provides an acceptable solution and the play-through speed can be adapted and paused to check for errors (see Figure 2.4). Each stage of the algorithm lights up as the program runs, allowing pupils to pinpoint each stage of the algorithm on the flowchart. Additional features allow for pupils to go on to create their own mimics to depict systems, simulations or games, as well as having the option of plugging in control boxes to create model-based simulations.

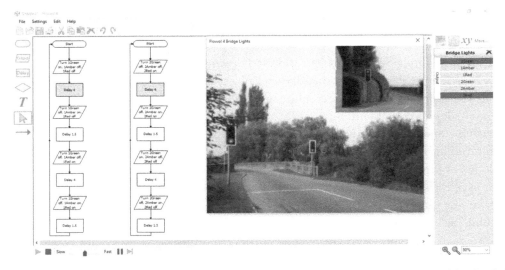

Figure 2.4 Flowol 4 Algorithm and traffic light simulation

Unplugged computational thinking

Many of the ideas discussed thus far can take place away from a computer. The teaching and learning of computer science concepts, through the use of games, props, puzzles and kinaesthetic approaches has gained popularity in recent years and has become known as 'unplugged' computing. As the name suggests, unplugged activities allow children and teachers to experience the concepts and approaches of computer science without the need for programming – and without requiring access to a computer (which even in today's technology-driven society should still not be assumed in the school setting). Unplugged activities, whether they are paper based, games or physical hands-on activities, can be particularly useful in explaining how computers systems and networks work using props or physical movements.

The University of Canterbury's (New Zealand) Computer Science Research Group introduced the Computer Science Unplugged Project and provides teachers with access to a range of open-source activities, available at: **http://csunplugged.org/** which can be copied, shared or modified.

Case study: unplugged computing with human robots

Emily is a trainee-teacher delivering a computing lesson to her Year 1 pupils which focuses on creating and debugging simple programs using the floor robot Bee-Bot. When planning the lesson, she recognises there is uncertainty regarding the children's prior knowledge of directional vocabulary. As a result, she incorporates an unplugged activity into her lesson to assess and develop this area before programming of the Bee-Bots.

Emily starts her lesson by taking children into the playground where a large maze is part of the permanent floor markings. Having briefed her teaching assistant, Mrs Smith, prior to the lesson, she deploys the services of Mrs Smith as a human robot. Emily guides the human robot through the maze using backward, forward, left and right commands. She switches between teacher and shared modelling to involve children in decision making when predicting steps and directions. Deliberate errors are made along the way to allow for debugging opportunities and Mrs Smith stays in role throughout to demonstrate that the robot will not correct errors or think for itself. Teacher modelling is followed by the shared writing of a program using arrows and numbers to depict the robot's journey.

Having modelled the activity, the children are split into groups of three to repeat the human robot activity. Emily explains the roles within each group as robot, programmer and recorder. Some groups manage to complete the maze with their human robots while others do not, but Emily is able to assess and provide guidance on directional language as well as the efficiency of their recording of instructions, before returning to class to begin programming of the Bee-Bots.

Post-lesson discussion between Emily and her university tutor provides evidence that this unplugged activity allowed pupils to develop several computational thinking skills, including the following:

- **Decomposition** – Pupils had to break down the task of completing the maze into smaller tasks for each stage of the journey.

- **Algorithms** – Pupils had to provide incorrectly ordered steps to their robot and had to evaluate and debug along the way.

- **Logical Thinking** – Pupils were making predictions and analysing the success of their programming throughout the task.

Computational thinking as a collaborative activity

There are several factors to consider when weighing up the benefits and limitations of whether pupils should work individually or collaboratively during computing activities. Assessment of individual computing knowledge, processes and skills (as opposed to the finished product or outcome) can prove challenging when pupils are working together and will be discussed further in Chapter 11, but there are clear benefits to pupils being afforded the opportunity to work both individually and collaboratively on computational thinking activities. Computational thinking includes several concepts which would gain from a collaborative approach, including pupils showing that they can share their reasoning and chosen approaches, as well as making evaluative judgements.

While computer networks are widely recognised as offering great potential for collaboration and communication, the portrayal of computer scientists by the popular media as socially awkward, introverted individuals who spend their days alone with their computer has done little to attract diversity within the technology sector. The development of group and paired teaching and learning approaches has been acknowledged as a key approach to programming education and the development of problem-solving skills (Ma *et al.*, 2004). By encouraging pupils to work together to solve problems and create solutions, pupils benefit from shared ideas and strategy, as well as having an extra pair of eyes to check and debug programming when required. Of course, effective group work needs careful planning, so pupils would benefit from clearly defined roles within the group and differentiation should also be considered. A hackathon approach, where groups of pupils can come together to collaboratively solve (or hack) a problem or create a game, app or product could also offer additional appeal and competition for some pupils.

Activity: developing efficiency through pattern recognition

This activity will enable you to identify the need for efficiency in computational thinking through the creation of a crystal flower pattern (also see Chapter 5) which utilises repeated code blocks in Scratch, a free visual programming language developed by the Lifelong Kindergarten Group at the MIT Media Lab. See **http://scratch.mit.edu**.

1. Go to: **https://scratch.mit.edu/projects/editor/**

   In the script area, create the following code to draw one square:

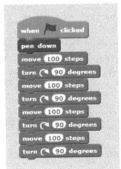 

Figure 2.5 Scratch script to draw a square

2. Having identified the repetition of instructions within the script for the drawing of the square, the script can be simplified as follows:

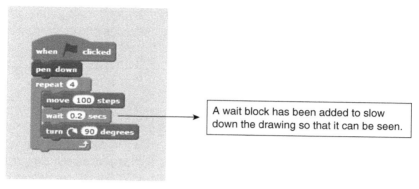

A wait block has been added to slow down the drawing so that it can be seen.

Figure 2.6 Scratch script to draw a square using repeat

3. Having created one square, a pattern can be created by repeating the square several times as the on screen sprite completes a full turn. To achieve a crystal flower pattern (see Figure 2.7 below), we can repeat the script above several times and turn the sprite each time to avoid

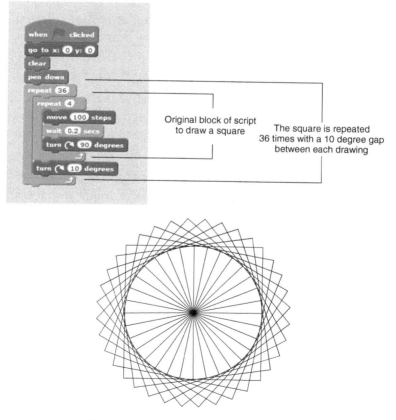

Original block of script to draw a square

The square is repeated 36 times with a 10 degree gap between each drawing

Figure 2.7 Scratch script to draw a crystal flower using repeated instructions

overwriting. However, this would not be an efficient approach and, having identified repetition in the pattern we are trying to create, the program above is far more effective.

4. Now use pattern recognition and repetition to create your own repeating pattern in Scratch. You may wish to start by using other regular polygons as your base pattern.

Learning outcomes review

This chapter has outlined how computational thinking is at the heart of the computing curriculum (DfE, 2013a) and explained the key processes and approaches which should be developed. Various approaches to computational thinking have been explored, including those using software and so-called unplugged approaches. It is clearly evident that computational thinking should not be viewed as a discrete skill and can be developed beyond the computing curriculum alone: cross-curricular approaches will be further explored in Chapter 9. Thinking about your current employer, school or training placement school, reflect on the questions below in relation to each learning outcome from this chapter.

- **Identify computational thinking as an essential skill which goes beyond the requirements of the computing curriculum.**
  In what ways would computational thinking processes help develop pupils' learning in other areas of the curriculum and school life?

- **Recognise the key processes and approaches involved in computational thinking.**
  Reflect on a recent computing lesson which you have planned and taught; which key computational thinking processes and approaches were the pupils developing?

- **Be familiar with approaches to computational thinking in the EYFS, KS1 and KS2.**
  Revisit the sections which discuss computational thinking in the EYFS, Key Stage 1 and Key Stage 2. Identify how the vocabulary used to outline curriculum expectations indicates the progression from one school phase to the next.

- **Identify ideas to incorporate unplugged activities into your lessons to develop computational thinking.**
  Reflect on a recent computer science lesson which you have planned and taught. Could the same lesson outcomes have been met through an unplugged approach? How could you include unplugged opportunities for computational thinking into the lesson?

Further reading and resources

Berry, M (2014) *Computational Thinking in Primary Schools*. Available at: **http:// milesberry.net/2014/03/computational-thinking-in-primary-schools/** (accessed 17 February 2017).

Miles Berry provides the historical context behind the shift from information and communication technology to computing and defines computational thinking.

Bird, J *et al.* (2014) Chapter 1 in *Lessons in Teaching Computing in Primary Schools*. Exeter: Learning Matters.

Chapter 1 of this book explores how to introduce algorithms and computational thinking to young children, including practical ideas for the classroom.

Computational Thinking Illustrated

Available at: **www.ctillustrated.com/download/**

(accessed 17 February 2017).

A set of cartoons which provide a stimulus for solving problems, designing systems, and understanding behaviours.

Computer Science Unplugged

Available at: **http://csunplugged.org/**

www.stem.org.uk/elibrary/collection/3909
(both accessed 17 February 2017).

Computer Science Unplugged provides free activities and resources that teach computer science through games and puzzles and active approaches, without requiring access to a computer.

Computing at School (CAS) Barefoot Computing Resources

Available at:

http://barefootcas.org.uk/barefoot-primary-computing-resources/concepts/ computational-thinking/ (accessed 17 February 2017).

The Barefoot Computing Project offers free in-school workshops for teachers and online teaching and learning resources. Online resources include explanations and every day examples of all computational thinking processes and approaches.

Google Computational Thinking Resources

Available at: **www.google.com/edu/resources/programs/exploring-computational- thinking/**

(accessed 17 February 2017).

Google's Exploring Computational Thinking (ECT) is a collection of lesson plans and resources for computational thinking. Videos show how computational thinking is used in everyday life and the technology industry.

The Scratch Guide to Computational Thinking

Available at: http://scratched.gse.harvard.edu/ct/index.html

(accessed 17 February 2017). Guidance on how computational thinking can be supported, developed and assessed through the use of the visual programming language, Scratch.

3 Programming with Floor Robots

Learning outcomes

By the end of this chapter you will:

- understand the pedagogical theories and practices of using floor robots to support teaching and learning;
- understand how floor robots can be used to engage children at different stages of learning;
- know how to program a floor robot and identify possible uses with children across the curriculum.

Teachers' Standards

A teacher must:

2. Promote good progress and outcomes by pupils:

- be aware of pupils' capabilities and their prior knowledge, and plan teaching to build on these.

3. Demonstrate good subject and curriculum knowledge:

- have a secure knowledge of the relevant subject(s) and curriculum areas, foster and maintain pupils' interest in the subject, and address misunderstandings.

4. Plan and teach well-structured lessons:

- contribute to the design and provision of an engaging curriculum.

5. Adapt teaching to respond to the strengths and needs of all pupils:

- know how to adapt teaching to support pupils' education at different stages of development.

(DfE, 2011)

Introduction

Although computing in the national curriculum (DfE, 2013a) may appear to be a 'new' area of learning, it is important to be aware of its antecedents in education since the late 1960s. You may already be familiar with floor robots, for example Roamer™ or Bee-Bots® (see Figure 3.1) and may have had experience of seeing these used or using them yourself with children. Floor robots can be programmed to move and change direction across the floor or a flat surface. Although the physical appearance of floor robots may be different, they function in a very similar way, the principles of programming them are broadly the same, and they have been used in schools as an educational learning tool for more than thirty years. It is worth briefly mentioning here that floor robots also use the same programming language as the screen turtle in Logo, which you will encounter in Chapter 5.

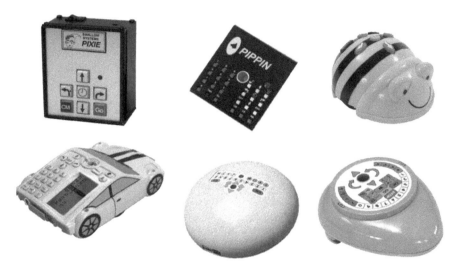

Figure 3.1 Floor robots. Top row, left to right: Pixie, Pippin, Bee-Bot. Bottom row, left to right: Pro-Bot, Classic Roamer, Roamer-Too

[Roamer is the registered trade mark of Valiant Technology Ltd.]

Research focus: discovery learning

Based on Piaget's notion of assimilation, Seymour Papert believed that the language of Logo could assist in helping children to develop and express mathematical ideas which they otherwise might find difficult in formal school contexts. Although children acquire language and speak naturally and easily, Papert recognised a lack of parity in the way children acquire understanding and competence in mathematics. He believed that this was not due to any inherent ability, but rather the conditions under which learning takes place. The teaching of mathematics in schools can often be impersonal, abstract and removed from children's experiences. Papert believed in Piaget's notion of *children as builders* in the sense that they create

⟶

their own intellectual structures and are able to learn *without being taught* but Papert then extends this analogy to include the notion of the kinds of *materials* that children need to build with (Papert, 1993:7). He argued that with formal mathematics there is both a shortage of materials and a cultural block that causes a phobia of mathematics in many people, both adults and children. Such a block prevents people from learning anything they see as mathematics, although conversely they may have no problem understanding something mathematical when they do not perceive it as such.

Discovery learning is very much about beginning with what the children already know or can do and in this sense is closely aligned with Piaget and constructivist theory which promotes the notion of child-initiated 'free play'. When working with children engaged in child-initiated 'play', you need to consider carefully how you will scaffold the situations to help them learn. This is usually achieved by directing children to work in pairs or small groups, with the understanding that they will be responsible for feeding back their findings or experiences to the rest of the class. This approach, ideally, achieves a balance between independent learning and autonomy, coupled with accountability, as even the youngest of pupils will have been briefed on the need to report their findings.

Floor robots in the EYFS

Before very young children are introduced to programmable toys, it is good practice to begin with concrete and physical activities first. At this age, children will have varying degrees of knowledge concerning conservation of number, the space around them and many will not yet have grasped an understanding of left or right. Their skills of estimating distances using units of any kind of measurement are most likely to be underdeveloped, and it is important to introduce these concepts one at a time.

Activity: spatial awareness

To begin with, work with small groups of children in a suitable space, for example in the hall or playground. Explain to them that they will be practising counting to 10 by taking steps forward together. To do this, hold the hands of a child either side of you, and tell them to do the same with the child next to them. Once the line has been formed, explain to the children that you are all going to take one step forward together. The point of this is to ensure all children take an equal step forward with one foot and then bring their second foot in line with their first. This may take some

(Continued)

(Continued)

practice until this movement becomes synchronised with all children in the group. Once children have learned this, then you can instruct them to take a given number of steps forward one step at a time counting with them as you go. This can then be extended to taking steps backwards.

During this activity, it is important not just to count and move with the children, but to be modelling the key words for them – *move, steps, forwards* and *backwards*. This activity may seem straightforward, but children as young as three will need time to practise and co-ordinate their gross motor skills, and this activity will need to be consolidated by repetition. It can then be extended by inviting the children in the group to predict how many steps it will take to reach a given point, for example, the door to the classroom or the climbing frame which will invite the use of positional language, e.g. near, nearer, nearest, further, farthest. Once children are comfortable with these notions of movement, space and distance, they can then be introduced to floor robots.

A note about floor robots

Floor robots may either look like insects or can be dressed up as animals. The reason for this is because it makes them visually appealing to young children. However, because floor robots appear to move and make noises independently, it is important to clear any misconceptions that the children may have about the floor robot being a living thing.

Activity: introducing floor robots

Begin by reminding children of their experiences of moving forwards and backwards in steps. Introduce the floor robot explaining that it can be programmed to do the same thing they did:

- Show them how to turn the floor robot on.
- Explain that the floor robot always remembers the last instruction it was given and show them how to clear the memory by pressing 'CLEAR' or with Roamer pressing the 'CM' button **TWICE**.
- Remind them of the steps they took when moving forward and explain the unit of distance – 1 unit = 1 length of the floor robot.
- Introduce the forward, backward and go buttons and model these (see Figure 3.2, below). For example, to move the robot forward 4 robot lengths (using the interfaces below), the program would be: CM CM ↑ ↑ ↑ ↑ GO, then: CM CM, before giving the robot the next instruction.

(Continued)

(Continued)

- Ask them to send the robot to each other.
- Allow them to experiment but be prepared to scaffold as necessary, for example, reminding them to clear the memory first or involve them in discussion about increasing/decreasing the units of distance. You can, when appropriate, show the children the 'PAUSE' or 'W' (wait) command. The 'wait' time is measured in seconds, so for example, to instruct the robot to pause for 5 seconds press the wait button five times.

Figure 3.2 Floor robot interfaces. Bee-Bot (left) and (right) Roamer-Too (EYFS interface)

Once children are confident to control the floor robot independently in a linear way, introduce the left and right commands. Although children may still not know their left from their right, the arrow icons allow visual association with the chosen direction. When modelling these commands, you will need to emphasise that the floor robot will not travel but will turn on the spot, and that by pressing the right command (→) twice, for example, the robot will complete two right turns to be facing the opposite direction. Another teaching point to emphasise is that commands can be entered then executed individually, or as a sequence. Either way, the 'clear memory' command will need to be entered before giving new instructions.

Using the floor robots will be exploratory where structures will be generated, tested, modified and combined and children will need time to assimilate what they are doing until it is 'owned'. In doing so, it is important that you model and encourage them to use the everyday language of position and distance (DfE, 2014). For any of the activities outlined in this chapter, or indeed, whenever working with floor robots, pupils will constantly be engaged in debugging their programs and refining them until they 'work'.

Although there are many commercial resources available, it can be useful for you to design your own to meet the needs of your children. Some starting points might be as follows:

- Using a sticky putty, attach messages, pictures or objects and program the floor robot to deliver these to someone.

- Create card games for the children to play. For example, a simple Bee-Bot race game can be organised with a start and finish line. Players take turns to pick a card from a stack and then follow the instruction on the card. These might just contain directional instructions, e.g. ↑ 4 or could include the 'wait' command to miss a turn. Laminating these cards will make them durable.

- Designing a route with the children for the floor robot to follow will allow you to determine the level of challenge, but will also provide the children plenty of opportunity to develop their skills of prediction and estimation.

- Floor robots are well suited to being embedded in story in an imaginative way. For example, stories such as Mairi Hedderwick's book, *Katie Morag Delivers the Mail* or Michael Rosen's *We're Going on a Bear Hunt* lend themselves to programming floor robots in a creative way. Children could be involved in designing and making a layout for the respective journeys using a range of art materials – in Katie's story planning a route around the Isle of Struay to deliver the mail, or in the bear hunt, journeying through forests and caves. In both cases, the stories and illustrations provide plenty of rich visual stimulus and will provide opportunities for children to develop both their programming and literacy skills.

Topic work in the EYFS offers scope for using floor robots creatively. For example, themes such as Pirates, Space and the Planets or Dinosaurs all allow opportunity to dress up the floor robot and to present learning in a meaningful context. Floor robots can also provide inspiration to support the teaching of phonics and early mathematics, which will be briefly covered later in this chapter.

Case study: reflecting on practice

Carrie is an Early Years PGCE trainee on a block placement in a Reception class. All trainees on the programme are required to evaluate their lessons. When her university tutor visited her in school, she shared this reflection with him:

In maths, the children have been learning about 2D shapes. The group I am with know the names of regular shapes and can talk about the properties of them. My mentor suggested they needed challenging and extending. The school's quite well resourced and they have some Bee-Bots and Roamers and because I'd used them at university, I thought they could program them to draw squares and rectangles. The children have used them through play and so I thought this would extend them, but my lesson didn't turn out as expected. My plan was to work in the hall with a group of six children in pairs, although at the last minute four more children came to join in, so I had ten. The Roamers have a pen holder in the middle and can

→

draw what they're programmed to do. You can do the same with the Bee-Bots, but you have to tape a pen to the back of them. Using paper on the floor, I thought the children could program them to draw a square and then as a challenge a rectangle. I began recapping the properties of squares and rectangles with the whole group and then modelled for them how to program making a square with Bee-Bots. The idea was they could get started while I showed AH, JD, BL and DS how to use the Roamer because the control panel is more complex. Before I started, I noticed that one pair of children had left their paper and equipment on the floor and were running around the hall. They wouldn't stop when I told them so I had to go over to get them back on task. After that, another pair said their Bee-Bot wasn't working and when I checked the batteries were dead, so I asked them to join another group. I managed to get back to the children with the Roamer but couldn't finish my explanation because another pair KL and MS needed my help. I could see some of the Bee-Bots weren't even on the paper, or if they were, they were drawing random lines and not squares, the children were over excited or arguing and the whole thing descended into chaos. AH, JD, BL and DS ended up not doing anything and in the end I had to stop the lesson.

Activity: lesson evaluation

In the case study given, consider the feedback that Carrie's university tutor might give her and the questions he might ask after reading her lesson evaluation. You may wish to record your points, observations or questions under different headings, for example: planning, resourcing, classroom management, subject knowledge, pedagogy, etc. Could this lesson have been successful? If so how, and if not, why not?

Using floor robots in Key Stage 1

Given the transition that takes place between the EYFS and KS1, you cannot assume that all pupils in Year 1 will have had the same experiences of programming or using floor robots as each other, and some may not have used them at all. Piaget's (1955) constructivist principles of starting with what the children already know will therefore be important. Some pupils may still need physical experiences of distance and space, whereas for others beginning with a simple floor robot would be appropriate. Assuming pupils have had experiences similar to those outlined in this chapter, then computational thinking and programming skills can be developed by introducing more complex commands using the Classic Roamer or the Infant Roamer-Too (see Figure 3.3).

The Classic Roamer is more sophisticated than some of the other robots such as the Bee-Bot. The number pad changes the way both the Classic Roamer and Roamer-Too are programmed to move or turn, and also introduces children to commands and concepts they will use when

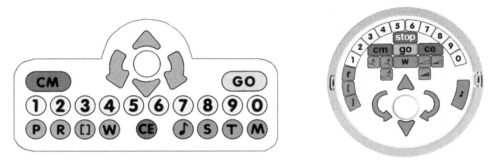

Figure 3.3 Classic Roamer interface (left); Infant Roamer-Too interface (right)

transferring their skills to using software and screen turtles. To begin with, children will need to know that for distance ① = 1 Roamer length, and that for direction numbers are used for the degree of turn. So, for example, to make Roamer go forward 3, turn right 90° and then go forward 6, the commands would be:

CM CM ↑ ③ → ⑨⓪ ↑ ⑥ GO

Most children in Key Stage 1 are unlikely to be familiar with using degrees to measure angle of turn and, to begin with, it may be best just to introduce '90' as the number needed to turn left or right. As children become more confident, they may want to be able to edit their commands before executing them, and by pressing the CE (clear entry) button they can cancel the previous entry. Both the Classic and the Infant Roamers introduce brackets and the R (repeat) command which helps children develop their pattern recognition skills. Programming the floor robot to create a square provides a useful way to demonstrate this. Using individual commands (known as primitives), the sequence for a 4 x 4 square would be:

CM CM ↑ ④ → ⑨⓪ ↑ ④ → ⑨⓪ ↑ ④ → ⑨⓪ ↑ ④ → ⑨⓪

In the instructions above, we have gone 'forward 4' and 'right 90' four times and the robot is back where it started. Floor robots are very good at carrying out repetitive tasks and using repeat (R) and brackets [ ] allows us to abbreviate the primitives used, so the algorithm this time would be:

CM CM R ④ [↑ ④ → ⑨⓪]

To explain this conceptual shift in programming to children, we can present this algorithm as a sentence: *Clear the memory twice, then do the following things four times: go forward four steps and turn right*. Similarly, repeat can be explained as the number of times of doing something and the brackets containing the list of things to do. Given that floor robots represent this with iconic language, they can be particularly effective in supporting pupils with EAL (Toh *et al.*, 2016).

Using floor robots in mathematics and geography

Activities outlined in the Early Years section can be adapted for children in Key Stage 1 although the formality of the classroom environment may have implications for planning and resourcing. In both Year 1 and Year 2, the national curriculum programmes of study for mathematics and geography align neatly with using floor robots.

In mathematics in Year 1, pupils use the language of position, direction and movement, including whole, half, quarter and three-quarter turns; and in geography, they use the four compass points for directions. To provide a real life and meaningful context, you (and the children) could create a map of the school to include a compass rose. If using Bee-Bots, for example, the map could be a grid of 15 cm squares (1 Bee-Bot length) and pupils could navigate the robot to different rooms or places and record the program including compass references e.g. ↑ ① (North), → ↑ ① (East).

Figure 3.4 Examples of 2D Shapes

In Year 2, the mathematics curriculum makes specific reference to using floor robots with instructions given in right angles (DfE, 2013c). Building upon their knowledge, for example, of writing programs to build a square or rectangle, pupils could work in small groups to create more complex 2D shapes. They could plan out these shapes by drawing them on squared paper first to help them identify the units of distance and where right angles of turn occur (see Figure 3.4). They could then use these drawings to assist with writing down the algorithm for the program and then ask another group to work out what shape it is from their code – which could also be achieved using squared paper.

In geography, pupils use the eight points of a compass, which provides potential to introduce 45° turns if using floor robots capable of this.

Assessment and pupil progress

As noted in Chapter 1, the Key Stage 1 computing curriculum places an emphasis on knowing what algorithms are and how to create, execute and debug them as programs. An important aspect of this is that children have practical experience of creating computer programs in order to solve problems (DfE, 2013a). This does not need to be long-hand as children can record and represent programs pictorially although introducing them to the correct Logo notation with floor robots, for example, 'FD 2' instead of ' ↑ ↑ ' (forward 2) and 'RT 90' instead of '→' (right 90) will assist them when using Logo (see Chapter 5).

Introducing activities which encourage children to record their thinking and reasoning will help provide you with evidence of their understanding of logic, algorithms and data representation (DfE, 2013a). This will also allow you to assess where children have or have not understood a concept or process (assessment in computing is covered later in Chapter 11). Much of the work that children do with floor robots will be exploratory and investigative in nature and there will often not be a finished piece of work as a result of the activity. However, Roamers and Pro-Bots both have pen holders which allows their movements to be recorded on paper and this can be useful in providing evidence of pupils' developments in programming. Alternatively, you may wish to agree and develop a system for writing or recording programs with the children. This can be as simple as using dots to predict or record each step of a floor robot's journey with a larger dot marking the starting point. Using this or a similar approach to recording will allow you to assess pupils' awareness and conceptual knowledge of left and right.

Research focus: learning about robots

This excerpt from Slangen et al. (2011), written just before the introduction of computer science into the national curriculum, goes to demonstrate why it is important to include floor robots in our school curriculum.

> In almost all sectors of society we encounter robotisation, that is, automated systems. In industry, robots weld, transport, assemble and paint. In medicine, sophisticated robots help to conduct complex surgery. Robots mow grass and clean swimming pools. Robots milk cows and steer ships. Military robots make bombs safe, explore hostile areas, and kill people. The robot is one of the fifty 'big ideas' in science and technology that should be known by everyone (Wisse, 2008), even by pupils (Gifford, 2005; Vanderborght, 2008). Many science and technology educators advocate that such big ideas should receive more attention in the school curriculum (Kipperman, 2009). Pupils themselves are well aware of the necessity of learning about robotics because of their likely ubiquitous presence in future society (Shin and Kim, 2007). Economic, technological and social perspectives urge schools to prepare pupils for robotics (Verlaan et al., 2007). Automated systems should be an item in the primary school curriculum (Boeijen et al., 2010). This justifies precious time in school being devoted to robotics (Slangen et al., 2011, p.450).

Before using floor robots or other control technologies with pupils in Key Stage 1, pupils could be asked to draw and label their idea of what a robot is and what it does. As part of wider discussion, pupils could be asked to identify examples of control technology around them, and how these are designed to make our lives easier.

Using floor robots in Key Stage 2

The use of floor robots in Key Stage 2 is generally less pervasive than in the earlier key stages, as much of the progression that occurs in terms of computational thinking and programming is replaced by the use of other programming tools (see Chapter 5). It is worth noting here that Roamer works with Scratch extensions (ScratchX) and that programs written in Scratch can be sent to a Roamer via Bluetooth (**www.roamer-educational-robot.com/roamer-works-with-scratch/**). Roamer-Too (see Figures 3.2, 3.3 and 3.5) provides a modular system with interchangeable interfaces which are designed to extend children's programming skills and can be used with children aged 3–18.

Classic Roamer and Roamer-Too include the function of being able to create **procedures** (P),which extends the use of the repeat command and brackets. Roamer-Too's additional features include adding inputs (such as light or movement sensors) and outputs (for example buzzers or motors), although to fully use these features you would need to add a control pod.

The Pro-Bot uses the same Logo technology as its sibling, the Bee-Bot, and can be programmed in the same way although units of distance are measured in centimetres, not robot lengths. The main advantage of the Pro-Bot over other floor robots is that when the keypad is used to enter commands, these appear simultaneously in the LCD written as Logo primitives which helps children assimilate the language they will encounter when programming a screen turtle.

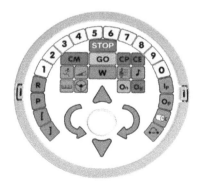 

Figure 3.5 Junior Roamer-Too interface (left); Pro-Bot interface (right)

The Pro-Bot also comes equipped with a light sensor on the bonnet and a sound sensor underneath. Sensors are also built into the front and rear bumpers and Pro-Bot can be programmed to respond to these inputs which can be turned on or off using the menu displayed in the LCD panel. They can then be programmed by editing an existing procedure, for example, 'when it goes dark' with options from the menu allowing you to select outputs such as turning the car lights on, which provides a stimulating way to introduce pupils to control technology. An easy-to-follow Pro-Bot user guide can be found here: **www. rmeducation.com/_rmvirtual/media/downloads/pro-bot_guide.pdf**

Case study: creative approaches to programming

As part of a primary education course, students created a video of a cross-curricular activity using Bee-Bots which involved choreographing a robot dance. The video can be viewed here: **https://www.youtube.com/watch?v=WmIokmEtpMg**

Activity

Although this video was made and produced by adults, how might you undertake a similar project with children in a Year 5 or 6 class? In doing so, consider the following:

- How long would a project like this take to plan and carry out?
- What are the different stages you would need to plan for?
- What different roles might the children take?
- What programming skills will the children need and how are these likely to be developed?

Using floor robots to support the teaching of literacy and mathematics

There are many videos on YouTube which provide examples of using floor robots to assist with the teaching of these areas. For example, learning letters and sounds:

www.youtube.com/watch?v=zGyLBzKR_VA&list=UUXop74UTLZ58Hhn7HJ9BCsg

or exploring number through playing a game:

www.youtube.com/watch?v=bxQZA4YHpbk

Key Stage specific resources

There are many available resources which are designed for floor robots to support learning across the curriculum. This section presents just a few examples:

EYFS

Bee-bots and EYFS activities on Pinterest **https://uk.pinterest.com/quirky2u/beebot-eyfs/**

This is primarily a picture catalogue but provides a source of ideas for using Bee-Bots. There are related boards, but you need to sign up for these.

Early Years teaching resources **www.earlylearninghq.org.uk/?s=bee-bot&search_cat=resource&x=0&y=0** offers a range of resources including Bee-Bot jackets and mats.

KS1

Phil Bagge at Code-it offers a useful Bee-Bot centred framework for delivering the computing curriculum including turtle progression, lesson ideas and printable activity cards.

http://code-it.co.uk/csplanning.html

Bee-Bot lessons provided by Focus Educational **https://www.focuseducational.com/product/bee-bot-lesson-activities-3/203** also offers a range of Bee-Bot accessories to assist teaching in KS1 including Bee-Bot mats. These are expensive but will give you an indication of how to use floor robots in a cross-curricular way.

KS2

A creative real-life case study of a Year 5/6 class using Roamer at Maple Cross Primary with a Star Wars theme can be found here: **http://roamerrobot.tumblr.com/post/47373232477/star-wars-roamer**

Teach Primary provide lesson ideas and activities for using floor robots linked to Ted Hughes' story *The Iron Man*.

www.teachprimary.com/learning_resources/view/lesson-ideas-for-control-technology

Road-themed Pro-Bot activity cards including activities such as 'bumper car' which uses touch sensors: **https://orchardgroveps.wikispaces.com/file/view/Probots+Learner+Cards.pdf**

Valiant Roamer Research Library

This provides a number of empirical research studies including the use of floor robots to support the teaching of computational thinking:

http://research.roamer-educational-robot.com/ as well as Kate Hudson's Valiant Blog which contains news and views about Roamer and educational robotics: http://katesblog. roamer-educational-robot.com/

Activity: evaluating resources

Considering the placement school and year group you are in, or will be going to, use the links above as a starting point to locate online resources. How might they be useful for teaching programming in a cross-curricular way? Using the link to Roamer library (above), what research evidence is there that using Roamer is beneficial in supporting the teaching of mathematical concepts?

A final note

Before planning to use floor robots with the children, it is worth remembering and noting the following:

- Floor robots work best on smooth, flat surfaces rather than carpets where friction slows them down.
- Children need to be trained to switch off the robots, and batteries will need to be checked or charged before use.
- Some children will need to orientate themselves behind the floor robot to operate it, whereas others will be able to operate it from any position.
- There are many phase-appropriate software programs and online resources which use screen turtles, but before using these children should, if possible, be conversant with using a physical turtle first. This is important because conceptually, on screen, ↑ ↓ represent up and down, rather than forward and back.

Learning outcomes review

In this chapter, you will hopefully have developed both your pedagogical and practical knowledge of floor robots and will have considered how their application in the classroom may vary from one age phase to another. From your reading and thinking

(Continued)

(Continued)

about the school where you are, respond to the questions or prompts which follow each of the intended learning outcomes as a means of identifying your knowledge and understanding of the issues covered in the chapter:

- **Understand the pedagogical theories and practices of using floor robots and the implications these have for teaching and learning.**
  In what ways has this determined how you plan learning experiences for children in the phase/year group where you were teaching? Provide examples from your practice to support how this has informed your teaching.

- **Understand how floor robots can be used to engage children at different stages of learning.**
  What evidence do you have to demonstrate that you have been able to differentiate the activities and features of floor robots to meet and support the range of need in your class?

- **Know how to program a floor robot and identify possible uses with children across the curriculum.**
  How can you demonstrate that you are familiar with programming floor robots, not just in the year group where you were teaching, but in the phases above and/or below? If there are gaps in your knowledge, how do you intend to address these?

- **Identify potential opportunities to use floor robots with learning in different curriculum areas.**
  What evidence do you have to demonstrate that you have used floor robots with children in different contexts or areas of the curriculum?

Further reading and resources

Berry, M (2015) *Computing at School (CAS) Quick Start Computing - A CPD toolkit for Primary Teachers*. London: Department for Education.

The CPD toolkit contains a wealth of useful information on all aspects computing and computational thinking from subject knowledge to planning and assessment. It also contains a comprehensive and highly useful knowledge and skills audit form.

Highfield, K (2010) Robotic toys as a catalyst for mathematical problem solving, *Australian Primary Mathematics Classroom*, 15 (2): 22–27.

Highfield provides a useful model in this paper for mapping floor robot activities to a classification of tasks in the early years and Year 1 (see pp.24–25).

Although the Classic Roamer and Roamer-Too can be programmed to play music, this chapter does not have the scope to explore these features although resources and activities can be found online from Valiant, the manufacturer: **www.valiant-technology.com/** as well as a Classic Roamer user guide **www.valiant-technology.com/uk/docs/Roamer_User_Guide.pdf**

(both accessed 17 February 2017).

A primary Roamer-Too keypad user guide can be found at: http://kcs4curriculum.co.uk/guidance-leaflets/roamer-leaflets

(accessed 17 February 2017).

4 Developing Programming through Age-Appropriate Software: KS1 Curriculum and Pedagogy

---

Learning outcomes

By the end of this chapter you should be able to:

- identify the KS1 curriculum requirements for programming;
- evaluate a range of software and tablet applications which introduce children to early programming skills;
- identify the learning theories which underpin common pedagogical approaches used in the teaching of programming;
- explore a range of pedagogical approaches which can be used to teach programming in KS1.

Teachers' Standards

A teacher must:

2. Promote good progress and outcomes by pupils:

- be aware of pupils' capabilities and their prior knowledge, and plan teaching to build on these.

3. Demonstrate good subject and curriculum knowledge:

- have a secure knowledge of the relevant subject(s) and curriculum areas, foster and maintain pupils' interest in the subject, and address misunderstandings;
- demonstrate a critical understanding of developments in the subject and curriculum areas, and promote the value of scholarship.

4. Plan and teach well-structured lessons:

- impart knowledge and develop understanding through effective use of lesson time;
- promote a love of learning and children's intellectual curiosity;
- contribute to the design and provision of an engaging curriculum within the relevant subject area(s).

(DfE, 2011)

Introduction

Programming is the result of code (or language) being used to represent an algorithm (a precise set of instructions) in a language which can be understood by a computerised system. When coupled with computational thinking, programming provides a way in which the solution to a problem can be actioned. Programming and coding have become interchangeable terms in recent years, with the latter gaining popularity in the media during the transition from the ICT programmes of study to computing in 2013. While these words may appear transposable, there are subtle differences between the two which can be misinterpreted or misconstrued. For example, in the Early Years, pupils' exploratory programming of digital devices such as floor robots may not necessarily be represented in code of any form. As children enter KS1, the code they will start to use to represent their algorithms will primarily be visual rather than text based.

This chapter builds upon both the unplugged approaches to computational thinking as outlined in Chapter 2, as well as the programming of floor robots in Chapter 3 by introducing the role of software and tablet applications in programming in KS1. This chapter will begin by identifying the role of programming in the KS1 national curriculum before looking at the origins of visual block programming software. Some common programming software tools and tablet applications for KS1 will be explored in this chapter, but due to the vast number of tools available, this chapter will also look at how teachers should evaluate such tools before selecting those which are most appropriate for their pupils. From a pedagogical perspective, this chapter will also explore the role of paired programming and scaffolding in programming with young children.

Programming in the Key Stage 1 computing curriculum

The national curriculum (DfE, 2013a) KS1 computer science requirements are as follows:

Pupils should be taught to:

- understand what algorithms are; how they are implemented as programs on digital devices; and that programs execute by following precise and unambiguous instructions;
- create and debug simple programs;
- use logical reasoning to predict the behaviour of simple programs.

It should be noted that these requirements can be fully met without pupils having to go anywhere near a computer, through unplugged approaches and the use of programmable devices. In addition, the requirements do not state that programs must be written or presented in a specific form. With this in mind, teachers should be confident using a range of approaches to teach programming, of which software and tablet applications should also be considered. In some schools, the approach which teachers take may be driven by the availability and timetabling of resources, but ideally the use of multiple approaches and resources allows pupils to develop and apply their knowledge, understanding and skills in a range of different contexts. The computing programmes of study also stress the importance of allowing pupils to have *repeated practical experience* (DfE, 2013a) of creating programs which allows understanding of computational thinking to be put into action.

Research focus: learning theories, block play and block programming

Children have always built, testing their theories about the physical and social world. They stack units, knock them down, enclose spaces, bridge gaps, and refine and repeat ideas. (Hewitt, 2001)

Scratch produced by the Massachusetts Institute of Technology's (MIT) Lifelong Kindergarten Group, is probably the most widely recognised and used programming platform in schools today. Its visual blocks which connect into place and its low-threshold – high-ceiling learning potential has been compared to the pedagogical approach of Friedrich Froebel's kindergarten which was based around block play (Berry, 2013a). Froebel's play-based, hands-on building and construction approach to learning has been identified as influencing Seymour Papert's later ideas on constructionism – learning by making, and the use of electronic blocks and software in the form of Logo, LEGO MindStorms and LEGO WeDo.

Figure 4.1 LEGO WeDo programming and controllable model

Papert's former colleague and doctoral student, Mitchel Resnick, recognised how Logo had fallen out of favour with teachers and pupils due to its complexity of syntax and lack of appeal – and has attempted to revive Papert's ideas through the introduction of Scratch (Resnick, 2013b). The Scratch user interface is built upon the same principle used in LEGO construction, allowing children to explore and tinker by snapping connecting bricks together.

Evaluating and choosing the right tools for programming in KS1

With the increased focus on computer science and programming in recent years, a wealth of software tools and tablet applications have been introduced onto the education market. This chapter can only scratch the surface in its exploration of the options which are available to teachers and pupils. While some teachers may prefer to use a range of tools for programming, there are greater benefits in allowing children the opportunity and time to develop their skills with one tool at a time. Before selecting a tool or application, teachers should explore the software themselves to evaluate and analyse how the tool will be used to meet curriculum and pupil needs.

A SWOT analysis approach could be taken to evaluate the strengths, weaknesses, opportunities and possible threats of the tool. Questions for teachers to consider may include:

- Why would this tool appeal to children?
- Which age groups is this tool most suitable for?
- Is it clear and easy to get started with the tool?
- Are help guides available?
- Is the tool accessible for all learners?
- Does successful use of the tool rely on children's skills or aptitude in other areas of learning?
- Is the tool open ended or does it reach a close where no further activities are possible?
- Can content be adapted by the user, for example, by uploading their own pictures or sounds?
- Can the tool be used in a collaborative approach?
- Does the tool promote computational thinking?
- Does this tool link to the requirements of the Key Stage 1 curriculum?

- Can this tool be used in a cross-curricular manner?
- What is the teacher's role when children are using this tool?
- How can pupil progress, and achievement be assessed and evidenced when using this tool?
- Could use of this tool present any online safety issues, for example, through advertisements, bias, copyright, inappropriate content or contact?

The table below lists some of the programming tools which may be suitable for pupils in Key Stage 1:

Table 4.1 Programming tools for KS1

Title	Platform	More Information and Cost
ScratchJr	iOS and Android	https://www.scratchjr.org/ Free
Daisy the Dinosaur	iOS	www.daisythedinosaur.com/ Free
Kodable	iOS, Android & Online	www.kodable.com/ Free (additional pricing options available)
LightBot	iOS, Android & Online	https://lightbot.com/ Free & Paid-for versions
Bee-Bot	iOS	www.tts-group.co.uk/tts-content/free-apps-for-our-floor-robots.html Free
LEGO WeDo	Hardware & PC/tablet Software	https://education.lego.com/en-gb/primary/explore See website for pricing
2Simple 2Code	Online (tablet friendly)	www.2simple.com/2Code Subscription-based content
TES iBoard	Online	www.iboard.co.uk/activities/subject/ict Free

Activity: evaluating a programming tool

Select and access one of the programming titles listed in the table above. (Your selection may be based on which platform or device is available to you.) Take time to explore the tool, considering how you would use it as a teaching tool, and how pupils may use it individually or in groups. Having explored the tool, go on to complete a SWOT analysis. The questions outlined above will help you to consider the strengths, weaknesses, opportunities and possible threats of the tool.

ScratchJr

Scratch programming language is intended for children of ages eight and over, and while it may also be used with younger children, the mathematical requirements and variety of options available in Scratch may be beyond the computing, mathematical and literacy skills of many Key Stage 1 pupils. The more recently launched ScratchJr provides a more suitable programming environment for younger pupils. ScratchJr is freely available on both Android and Apple iOS platforms, and additional teaching and learning resources can be found on the accompanying website (see further resources at the end of this chapter).

ScratchJr uses programming blocks to make chosen onscreen events happen. The user interface bears some similarities with Scratch – in its use of the green flag to execute programs, the background stage and the cat sprite as the default character – but one key difference is in its range and presentation of programming blocks to create programming script. Scratch consists of ten programming block categories: motion, looks, sound, pen, data, events, control, sensing, operators and add-in blocks. Each of these categories contains several blocks which can be connected to create a program of script.

In ScratchJr, the number of block categories is reduced to covering the following options (starting from the top row in Figure 4.2) – Triggering blocks, Motion, Looks, Sounds, Control, End Blocks.

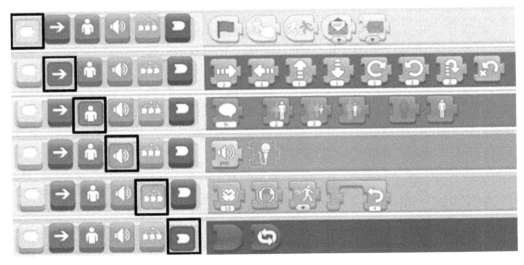

Figure 4.2 ScratchJr programming block categories

ScratchJr is a collaborative creation between the DevTech Research Group at Tufts University, the Lifelong Kindergarten Group at the Massachusetts Institute of Technology Media Lab, and the Playful Invention Company (see **http://scratchjr.org**, DevTech Research Group, 2016).

This reduction in categories provides a user environment which is more approachable for KS1 pupils and removes categories which are in line with KS2 curriculum areas such as data, operators and sensors. Despite the reduced programming block options of ScratchJr, it still provides an open-ended platform for programming. This allows children to interact with programming in a self-directed exploratory style using the time-honoured kindergarten pedagogical approach (Bers *et al.*, 2015), but can also be used in a more structured manner to meet the requirements of the computing curriculum, as can be seen in the following case study.

Case study: Year 2 children using ScratchJr to recreate a playground game

This case study explores how Amina, a newly qualified teacher, used ScratchJr with her Year 2 pupils.

Amina's initial teacher training covered computing. She recalled one particular workshop where, along with her peers, the computing lecturer had taken the group outside to play a game of tag. The lecturer then showed the trainee teachers an algorithmic representation of the playground game in the form of a flowchart, which depicted the procedural approach towards playing the game and the decisions which players had to make. A year on, and with a class of her own, Amina used this idea with her Year 2 pupils, which resulted in children creating their own tag games using ScratchJr.

Figure 4.3 A Year 2 child's ScratchJr script for a simple tag game

→

Amina started the unit of work in computing ensuring that children understood the rules and procedure for playing the game. She achieved this by providing the opportunity for the children to play the game, taking photographs of key points of the game. The photographs supported children's understanding of the game and together a shared algorithm in the form of a set of instructions was created.

Children had already used ScratchJr in Year 1, but they had not created programs in which one character's actions impacted on another's; therefore, this became the key teaching focus for this unit and pupils were introduced to how the triggering programming blocks could be used to show how characters interact with each other during the game. In the screenshot above (Figure 4.3), one child's programming shows that when one character runs into another, a 'Tagged!' speech bubble appears.

Amina's evaluation of the computing unit of work was very positive and she recognised that over the course of the sequence of activities, pupils created and implemented their algorithms in the form of programming. They had also utilised debugging skills and used a range of problem-solving skills to design and test their programs.

Bee-Bot tablet application

Earlier in Chapter 3, we were introduced to our friend the Bee-Bot – a programmable digital device in the form of a floor robot. In this section, we will take a look at the Bee-Bot tablet application (The TTS Group, 2016) which provides an onscreen simulation of the Bee-Bot. The Bee-Bot tablet application is a free application available on the Apple iOS platform. Similar to Logo and other onscreen robot (or turtle) software, the Bee-Bot application requires the user to control the robot by using programming to move the robot to a specific location. The Bee-Bot application uses the same input keys as the robot version, therefore providing familiarity for pupils. In addition, the application also makes use of sequential memory where new commands are added to previous programming unless the memory is cleared.

While Bee-Bot robots may present greater opportunity for directional language to be developed in an active and physical manner, the two-dimensional nature of the Bee-Bot application may expose misconceptions around direction and positioning. Such misconceptions should not cause concern and need to be treated as learning and assessment opportunities to show that children are able to translate understanding between different contexts and platforms.

The Bee-Bot application provides a range of challenges presented in a game style where the user has to program the onscreen Bee-Bot to a given finish position. Having completed a challenge the user is informed of the completion time and rewarded stars accordingly, with challenges becoming progressively more difficult as the user progresses through the game levels. The application is colourful and appealing for children, and provides context for programming (similar to that which can be achieved through the use of Bee-Bot robot mats).

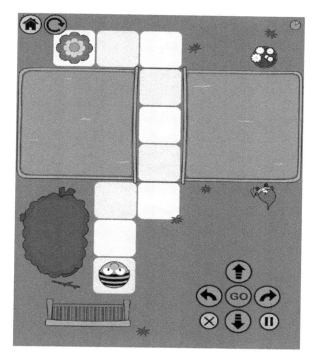

Figure 4.4 Example Bee-Bot application activity (challenge 7 of 12)

In this activity (Figure 4.4), the user is required to program the Bee-Bot from its starting position to reach the flower.

This can either be achieved in one complete program or several smaller programs where the memory would need to be cleared before new programming can inputted.

Activity: planning for teaching and learning with the Bee-Bot application

Like many education-based programming applications, the Bee-Bot application presents a challenge-mode approach which the user can work through at their own speed. As a result, teachers would need to consider how the use of this tool can be incorporated in programming lessons.

Any teacher planning to use the Bee-Bot application in their classroom would need to consider several factors before implementing its use. If you were using the Bee-Bot application with KS1 pupils, consider the approach which you would take based on the areas outlined below:

(Continued)

(Continued)

Questions to consider:

- How could the Bee-Bot application be used during teacher-led input?
- If pupils are using the application individually or in small groups, what role could the teacher take?
- How can programming requirements be differentiated for pupils who may struggle to remember the Bee-Bot steps in one go?
- Which additional resources could be used to support pupils in remembering and recording the programming steps they input?

The Bee-Bot application tracks how quickly each user completes a specific challenge and rewards stars accordingly. While this approach may motivate and engage some pupils, other forms of assessment need to be considered.

- Which assessment strategies could be used to ascertain pupil progress and achievement when using the Bee-Bot application?
- In relation to the Key Stage 1 national curriculum computing requirements, which aspects of programming and computational thinking can be assessed through this application?
- How can teachers provide evidence to support their assessment of pupil progress and achievement when using the Bee-Bot application?

Case study: programming with LEGO WeDo

This case study focuses on a group of primary trainee teachers who planned and ran a half-day workshop for Year 2 and 3 pupils using LEGO WeDO.

LEGO WeDo is a resource made up of hardware and software which can be used by children to build and program robots. LEGO WeDo can be viewed as the Kindergarten version of LEGO Mindstorms and is intended for children of approximately five to eight years of age. Each LEGO WeDo kit can be used by a group of pupils to create a specific model which can then be programmed using the accompanying visual block-based programming software.

Four trainee teachers who had chosen to specialise in Primary computing were given the role of planning and delivering a workshop to a group of Year 2 and 3 pupils. The trainee teachers wanted to use a hands-on approach during the workshop and decided that LEGO WeDo would provide both learning opportunities for computational thinking and programming, as well as provide an engaging resource and context for learning.

The workshop begun with children being introduced to the story of *The Crocodile under the Bed* (Kerr, 2015) to engage and capture interest, before children were shown a crocodile made

$\longrightarrow$

of LEGO WeDo, complete with motion sensor and motor-operated jaw (see Figure 4.1). The construction of the crocodile was explained as an algorithmic process before children were split into groups of 3 and followed onscreen step-by-step instructions to make their own LEGO crocodiles. Including the trainee teachers, the class's teacher and teaching assistant, there were six adults in the room. This meant that adults were able to facilitate learning through discussions and questions in a manageable manner.

Having created their models, which took around 30–40 minutes, groups moved on to programming their robots by following script which has already been suggested within the software. This code-tracing approach was an appropriate starting point for children before moving on towards adapting programs and introducing their own ideas.

At the end of the workshop, pupils were asked to evalaute and one child commented: *Our model didn't work at first and we had missed some parts. We went to the instructions and got it right. We made the program non-stop by putting a loop on it. We changed the numbers so that we got different sounds.*

The trainee teachers were also asked to evaluate the workshop and they suggested the following tips for the use of LEGO WeDo kits:

- Groups of three work well as there is a role for everyone: maker, checker and resource handler.

- Ensure children work within the box to avoid LEGO pieces going missing or ending up in the wrong kit.

- Don't rush to help if the models don't work: allow children to use their debugging skills.

- Making the models takes time, but it's important that children make the models to be able to follow an algorithm and understand how the models work.

- Following ready-made code may be a good starting point, but ensure pupils have the opportunity to use their own programming ideas and skills.

Lightbot™ tablet application

Lightbot, Lightbot Jr and Lightbot Code Hour (Yaroslavski, 2016) are tablet applications which introduce programming concepts through a game-based approach, where users are required to navigate an onscreen robot around a square and cube maze and switch on lights. Originally created as a Flash game, Lightbot is now available on both Android and Apple iOS platforms with the Lightbot Code Hour Application providing a free introductory trial of the tool.

Lightbot starts by introducing users to programming basics to get the robot moving, turning, jumping and switching on lights. As the user progresses through the levels or challenges, more complex concepts such as procedures and loops are introduced for older children or those who are ready. Programming remains visual throughout and the user can adapt and test algorithms along the way without the need to start over. Like other programming tablet applications, Lightbot quickly progresses in its level of challenge and only the initial stages may be appropriate for KS1 pupils, but used correctly and supported by pedagogical approaches which encourage quality dialogue and appropriate scaffolding, Lightbot promotes an intuitive approach where efficiency and perseverance are developed.

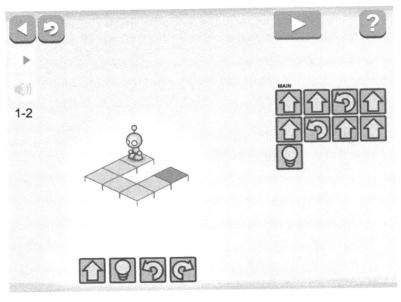

Figure 4.5 LightBot Code Hour: Programming Basics

Figure 4.5 shows an example of one of Lightbot's programming challenges, where the user is required to program the robot around the maze to the shaded tile which needs to be lit up. Programming script shows that the following algorithm is required:

- Two steps forward
- One anticlockwise turn
- Two steps forward
- One anticlockwise turn
- Two steps forward
- Switch lightbulb on

As the user executes the program, each stage of programming is highlighted so that each stage of the algorithm can be linked to the actions of the robot and errors identified. In further levels, users are required to select the most efficient routes as the number of programming steps becomes restricted. This is also the stage when users are ready to recognise the need for procedures and loops.

Kodable programming curriculum

The Kodable Programming Curriculum (SurfScore Inc., 2016) is one of the few programming applications which offers teachers additional controls and tools to track progress through different levels of programming. Kodable is free to use online or on iOS or Android platforms, although schools can purchase additional levels, administration access, curriculum planning and professional development content if desired. Having created a teacher account on the Kodable website (**https://www.kodable.com/**) teachers can create classes, add pupils and track and manage the levels at which pupils are using the tool.

Kodable is beautifully colourful, appealing and intuitive to use. The concept is centred around The Fuzz Family – a group of fuzzy-ball type characters. The user must guide the characters through a series of mazes by correctly programming the pathway using directional arrows. When the program is executed, the fuzz-ball character rolls along the selected pathway, collecting reward coins and gaining points along the way. Kodable is for users aged five and upwards, and early programming skills are developed in the so-called Smeeborg area of Kodable, where users work their way through a sequence of progressively more challenging activities, before conditions and loops are introduced. Figure 4.6 shows an example of a Kodable activity which builds upon understanding of sequencing by introducing the user to

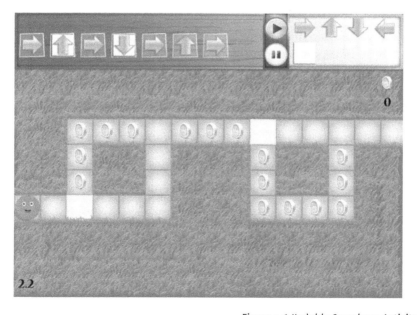

Figure 4.6 Kodable Smeeborg Activity: Conditions

conditions ('if this, then that' statements). In the example above, if the fuzz ball rolls onto a highlighted coloured square a specific action must be performed – in this case a change of direction.

In each level of Kodable, there is ample opportunity for users to consolidate and apply their understanding although teachers may find that the repetitive nature of the activities may not appeal to all pupils. Therefore, it is highly recommended that teachers do create a teacher account to enable greater selection over which materials are used and how, as well as enabling access to lesson plans, ideas and videos which explain computing concepts.

Scaffolding in programming approaches in Key Stage 1

Scaffolding, as first defined by Bruner *et al.* (1976), describes the role of the teacher in assisting a child to meet the desired learning outcome. Similar to Vygotsky's (1978) zone of proximal development, scaffolding utilises interaction between teachers and pupils, and potentially pupils and their peers to bridge the gap between what is known and what is not yet known. Scaffolding consists of a step-by-step process where supporting strategies and structures are in place during the initial stages of learning new concepts, and then later removed as expertise develops.

Modelling is a commonly used scaffolding strategy by teachers and its importance should not be underestimated in computing lessons. When introducing a new programming tool to pupils, it is essential that teachers 'think out loud' when modelling its use to pupils. This allows pupils to begin to understand the underlying thought processes in use and reasoning behind decisions which are taken. In the case of ScratchJr (see Figure 4.3), teacher modelling in the form of 'thinking out loud' could be used to explain how and why certain blocks are used, and deliberate errors could be made to show that debugging is a part of the programming process.

Other scaffolding strategies in computing may include the use of code-tracing. Code-tracing is where a pupil is given pre-written code to complete or copy. This may be beneficial in offering a supportive scaffolding approach for young programmers, for example, where programming software may be dependent on a child's literacy skills, such an approach would allow the child to focus on their understanding of the algorithm and the requirements of the program rather than the syntax. Similarly, code-hacking (or seeing inside the program), where a pupil is given a completed program to understand, remix (adapt) or correct is another approach which can provide an alternative to programming where a child's progress is not just based on their ability to input code. In choosing scaffolding strategies, teachers will need to weigh up the benefits, against potential incidental learning and debugging opportunities which may be missed.

Paired programming

In a study of 357 primary and secondary teachers in England, Sentance and Csizmadia (2015) identified that one of many pedagogical approaches used by teachers in computing was a collaborative working approach. This included team work, peer mentors, paired programming and collaboration, with teachers recognising the positive affect of collaborative approaches in pupils' motivation and engagement.

Paired programming is an approach to programming which originates from software development companies. During paired programming, two programmers work on the same programming project at the same computer. During the project each individual takes either the role of 'driver' or 'navigator'. The driver controls the mouse and keyboard and leads on inputting the code, while the navigator reviews the code, makes suggestions and identifies errors (Williams and Kessler, 2000). Paired programming supports in transforming the image of computer programming from being a lonely individual activity towards recognising the benefits of collaborative programming. In research conducted by the National Center for Women and Information Technology (2009), the benefits of paired programming among American computer science undergraduates were identified as:

- improved student performance and retention;
- increased confidence for all students, including a reduction in the confidence gap between female and male students;
- development of critical thinking skills;
- providing a real world/workplace working environment.

Much of the research relating to programming originates from an industry or Higher Education background, however, paired programming is beginning to gain prominence in secondary schools too. Franklin (2016) suggests that paired programming in schools should be adapted and the roles of driver and navigator should be avoided to ensure collaboration is on equal terms. He also recommends that pairs are made up of children with similar abilities in computing, or at least children who perceive themselves to be of equal ability. While mixed-ability pairing may work, it is essential that the children can work productively and in a supportive manner. The use of two keyboards for each computer is encouraged to increase participation, although the use of a timer may be required to avoid confusion and share control of input equally.

There is little research which looks at the use of paired programming in primary classrooms, but this approach to teaching and learning can certainly be adapted for younger pupils. In many primary schools, there is already a common practice in place where pupils share hardware devices, often as the outcome of resource or timetabling implications, therefore paired programming could be implemented to provide greater structure and substance to the collaborative working which may already be in place. As with any collaborative approach, teachers will need to consider how individual performance can be assessed and built upon from one lesson to the next.

Activity: assessment of paired programming

Having learned about paired programming, consider your approach to assessment in such paired activities.

- What are the challenges of assessing pupil work or progress in computing?
- If pupils are working in pairs, which assessment strategies could you deploy to assess individual learning and progress?
- What are the pros and cons of keeping the same paired programming partners for a sustained period of time?

Learning outcomes review

This chapter has explored programming tools and approaches which could be used in KS1. It can be seen that a whole host of educational programming tools and applications have been launched in recent years, which can be both exciting and confusing for teachers. With this is mind, this chapter recommends that teachers explore and evaluate such tools before putting them in the hands of pupils, and to consider the teaching and learning strategies which will be used to develop pupils' understanding of programming and not just the tool. Programming in KS2 will be considered in the next chapter. Thinking about a school with which you are familiar, reflect on the questions below in relation to each learning outcome from this chapter.

- **Identify the Key Stage 1 curriculum requirements for programming.**
  Using schemes of work and/or medium-term planning from your school, identify where and how the national curriculum Key Stage 1 computer science requirements are delivered. Is there progress in expectations from Year 1 to 2?

- **Evaluate a range of software and tablet applications which introduce children to early programming skills.**
  What are the key factors to be considered when choosing a programming tool for Key Stage 1 pupils?

(Continued)

(Continued)

- **Identify the learning theories which underpin common pedagogical approaches used in the teaching of programming.**
  Find out how block play is used in the Early Years classrooms within your school. If possible, observe pupils or talk to teachers to identify the skills which children develop through their use of the blocks. Identify any crossover between the skills needed for block play and those for programming.

- **Explore a range of pedagogical approaches which can be used to teach programming in Key Stage 1.**
  With your class (or most recent class) in mind, reflect on the potential benefits and challenges of implementing a paired programming approach.

Further reading and resources

Froebel Gifts

Available at: **http://froebelgifts.com/resources.htm** (accessed 17 February 2017).

A website dedicated to Friedrich Froebel's educational philosophy, methods and resources.

Paired Programming

Available at:

https://www.ncwit.org/resources/pair-programming-box-power-collaborative-learning

https://www.axsied.com/pair-programming/

(both accessed 17 February 2017).

Background information and guides for implementing paired programming in the class. Although intended for older students, teachers may find these resources useful in understanding the benefits of paired programming and drawing on the advice and tips of educators who have tried it for themselves.

Playground Games Flowchart Algorithms – Phil Bagge

Available at:

http://code-it.co.uk/unplugged/playgroundgames/playgroundoverview

(accessed 17 February 2017).

Phil Bagge's playground game algorithms are great unplugged activities which can be used as they are or developed further into animations or games which pupils can create using programs such as ScratchJr.

Times Educational Supplement – Interactive Resources (on screen control/programming). Available at:

www.iboard.co.uk/activities/subject/ict (accessed 17 February 2017).

Despite slightly dated reference to the old ICT curriculum, these free activities provide an alternative to applications such as Bee-Bot where the user must control an on screen robot to achieve a particular goal.

One Key Logo

Available at:

http://scratch.redware.com/project/one-key-logo

http://scratch.redware.com/project/one-key-logo-play-button (both accessed x February 2017).

The specific syntax requirements of MSW Logo as discussed in Chapter 5, will prove too challenging for many KS1 pupils. This version of Logo created in Scratch, is made specifically for younger pupils, requiring only one letter instructions such as F for Forward, B for Back, R for Right and L for Left, to enable the sprite to draw lines on screen.

5 Developing Programming through Age-Appropriate Software: KS2 Curriculum and Pedagogy

Learning outcomes

By the end of this chapter you should be able to:

- identify the Key Stage 2 curriculum requirements for programming;
- use and evaluate a range of software which builds upon children's skills knowledge and concepts of programming;
- demonstrate your own knowledge of how to use different software programs to teach the computing curriculum at KS2;
- identify ways in which pupils and teachers can work together to support the development of programming in KS2.

Teachers' Standards

A teacher must:

2. Promote good progress and outcomes by pupils:

- be aware of pupils' capabilities and their prior knowledge, and plan teaching to build on these.

3. Demonstrate good subject and curriculum knowledge:

- have a secure knowledge of the relevant subject(s) and curriculum areas, foster and maintain pupils' interest in the subject, and address misunderstandings.

4. Plan and teach well-structured lessons:

- promote a love of learning and children's intellectual curiosity;
- contribute to the design and provision of an engaging curriculum within the relevant subject area(s).

5. Adapt teaching to respond to the strengths and needs of all pupils:

- know when and how to differentiate appropriately.

(DfE, 2011)

Introduction

This chapter builds upon the approaches to developing children's experiences, skills and knowledge of programming in Key Stage 1 outlined in Chapter 4. It also builds upon concepts and processes covered elsewhere in this book, for example, using floor robots in Chapter 3 is extended here to develop programming concepts with MSW Logo. Children's experiences of using ScratchJr covered in Chapters 2 and 4 are developed with Scratch 2.0 and the use of Kodu and Python, as alternative programming platforms, are also briefly explored. From a pedagogical point of view, consideration is given to the use of text and block-based scripts to meet the needs of different learners. The research focus in this chapter explores pupil-teacher partnerships and the notion of pupils as digital leaders.

Programming in the Key Stage 2 computing curriculum

The national curriculum Key Stage 2 computer science requirements are as follows:

Pupils should be taught to:

- design, write and debug programs that accomplish specific goals, including controlling or simulating physical systems; solve problems by decomposing them into smaller parts;

- use sequence, selection, and repetition in programs; work with variables and various forms of input and output;

- use logical reasoning to explain how some simple algorithms work and to detect and correct errors in algorithms and programs;

- create a range of programs, systems and content that accomplish given goals.

(DfE, 2013a)

Engaging pupils with the above requirements can be achieved using age-appropriate educational software which is freely available online – and ought not to be constrained by the need to purchase additional apps, equipment or peripherals. However, much will depend upon the resources which are available to you in the schools where you are teaching. Depending upon their scheme of work (SoW), pupils' experiences of controlling systems may involve the use and construction of physical components such as LEGO WeDo or RoboLab. There are many benefits which accompany this approach: the main one being that they provide children with tactile experiences of creating models which they can then control by programming the software that comes with them. However, due to the costs involved, there are many schools which elect to use software or other approaches that provide pupils with virtual experiences of *controlling or simulating physical systems* (DfE, 2013a).

Scratch 2.0

In Chapter 4 you encountered ScratchJr which introduces programming through the context of stories, images and scenarios. It also introduces children to using simple block code and different sprites which can be programmed to move and tell a story.

Scratch 2.0 (MIT, 2016a) is designed for 8-11 year olds and beyond, although the general feel and look of the program will be familiar if they have used script blocks in ScratchJr. Scratch is rooted in the MIT tradition of Logo (see next section) and built upon many of its concepts, but takes advantage of new computational ideas and capabilities to make it easier for children to get started with programming. The use of counters within script blocks also allows children to become familiar with controlling a wide range of numerical settings. For example, children can evidence how many times a sprite repeats doing a certain thing. Scratch 2.0 is free to use online or available to download to your computer **https://scratch.mit.edu/** or as an app for iOS and Android. However, you should always seek the advice of your mentor before downloading any software (even on your phone!) while in school.

Getting started with Scratch

Figure 5.1 (below) gives an overview of the features of Scratch 2.0, which may provide a useful reference point when introducing the program.

One possible place to start is by getting children to create their own sprite, as Scratch has a built-in paint program where the suite of editing tools is likely to be familiar to the children. A range of sprite characters can be created or chosen from the sprite library. Demonstrating how the sprite moves and behaves introduces the script blocks (see Chapter 4 p.48) and how they can be added, swapped and moved around. Children will need to be shown how to edit counters and will need to get a feel for units of movement, distance, positioning with x and y coordinates and using negative numbers. While experimenting with code, if the sprite 'disappears' then it can be dragged back to centre stage or set manually (the x:0 y:0 coordinates of the cat sprite equates with a point just above its right elbow).

Scratch tutorials and projects

The help menu allows you to select different tutorials which provide a practical way to develop skills, as well as learning different script blocks and working with multiple sprites. They do require a certain level of reading but the screenshots and short videos demonstrate how to code visually – and you can switch easily between your code and these materials which can be adapted to suit your needs. Backgrounds and sprites can be imported and customised and the games children create can be programmed to make them more difficult to play (by changing the size and speed of the sprites) as well as more sophisticated by including timers, sensors and score counters.

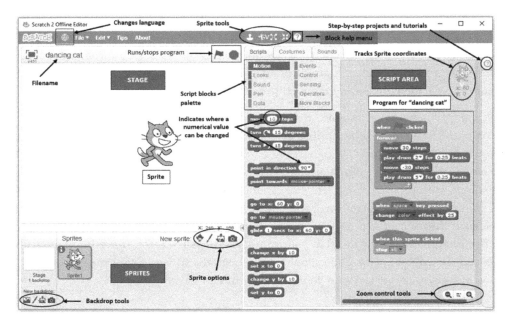

Figure 5.1 Annotation of Scratch 2.0 Interface

The level of complexity in programming generally progresses between tutorials, and by working on projects which vary in nature, different features of the program can be explored. For example, those involving music and dance may draw mainly upon the motion, looks and sound scripts, whereas creating a game might involve scripts using sensing to trigger events and data blocks to create variables. Even at a basic level, using the control script blocks introduces the programming concepts and language of loops using the "repeat" or "forever" command as well as using conditional statements such as "if… then" (for example, if the cat sprite is clicked then it will meow).

Working with scripts

As part of your role as a teacher, you will need to try out scripts and projects to see how things work as well as tinkering with and debugging the algorithms yourself. It is one thing to blindly copy code and another to understand what it does and, therefore, knowing how the script works is vital. Regardless of what or how you teach, the children need to understand and explain what the code does – which holds true for whatever programming language you use. Scratch 2.0 is user-friendly in this sense as the block help menu (see Figure 5.1) allows you to click on code to reveal what it does.

Not only will children need to know what scripts do in programming terms, they will also need to be secure with the mathematical concepts involved. For example, a game which uses the arrow keys to navigate a sprite will require some knowledge of the four quadrants and negative coordinates.

A note about games

With the teaching of Scratch in Key Stage 2, there may be a focus on gaming and so much of what children learn in programming will be through making games, which Scratch is well suited to doing. Getting children involved in planning their games (see Chapter 8) is not just important in terms of design and the purpose of the game, but also in working out what code will be needed, and what it will do. Studying the genre of game platforms can be useful in helping pupils decide and plan what game they are going to create and also introduces designing a game stage (for example a maze) and creating costumes and costume changes to animate sprites. The code-it website **http://code-it.co.uk/** contains some good materials which are useful if you are coding with a games theme (see further resources).

Activity: making a Scratch game

Using one of the existing projects in the tutorial, create a game (a Race, Pong, Hide and Seek or Catch). Have a go at customising the game's appearance by importing your own background and editing your sprites. See if you can add a variable (data script block) to create a score board and/or game time counter. During the process consider the following:

- What did you need to tinker with and why?
- How much time was spent debugging your program as opposed to creating it?
- What did you need to debug and how did you get it working?
- If you were planning to teach children how to create this game, what things would you need to consider?
- Are you sure you understand your code? Write an explanation of what each part of the code does which could be understood by children.

Scratch with other programs

As already mentioned in Chapter 3, Roamers can execute programs written in Scratch. Similarly, LEGO WeDo 1.0 and 2.0 (see Chapter 4) can be used to run programs by going to 'more blocks' then 'add an extension'. These provide sound, practical ways of demonstrating engagement with the computing programme of study which refers specifically to controlling or simulating physical systems (DfE, 2013a).

There is also potential to make links between using the features of Scratch which are akin to those in Logo. For example, the creation of shapes and patterns in Logo can also be achieved in Scratch (see Chapter 2). Making a game or animation which involves a sprite leaving and/or hiding their trail also makes good use of the pen and control blocks.

Advanced use of Scratch can also link to work that pupils may have done with HTML and web design, and various content and online media can be created using Scratch scripts: **https:// scratch.mit.edu/projects/70150790/**

A final note on Scratch

Scratch 2.0 provides an open-ended on- or off-line programming platform which is well resourced with plenty of support materials, activities and starting points. You will need to sign up to access some of these and once subscribed you can also share your own projects online.

The main advantages of Scratch 2.0 over Logo, is that it is bright, colourful and appealing to children and offers an intuitive and accessible way to combine multimedia into their programming projects. However, when moving children on from working with blocks to writing their own text-based scripts, Logo provides an appropriate educational tool. Developing children's knowledge of working with shapes, space and patterns is something which Logo does particularly well.

Microsoft Windows [MSW] Logo

As outlined in Chapter 3, Logo is a software program which translates the concept and movement of the floor robot into the virtual world of the screen turtle which, like a floor robot, can be programmed. There are many different versions of Logo used in the primary classroom, for example, One Key Logo (see Chapter 4), Black Cat Logo and Roamer World. Their appearance and interface may vary, but essentially the programming language they use is the same, although there may be occasional discrepancies between commands. Unlike some versions of the program, the MSW Logo (Softronics Inc., 2016) screen turtle takes the form of a triangle rather than the physical appearance of a turtle. MSW Logo is free to download (**www.softronix.com/logo.html**).

Getting started with Logo

Pupils may have had experience using floor robots in Key Stage 1 but they may be unfamiliar with the screen equivalent, and for this reason it is important to address potential misconceptions:

- Rather than travelling distance in units of robot length, the Logo turtle travels in screen pixels and so children will need to work with larger numbers. For example, entering the command to move forward 100 will result in the turtle travelling about 2.5cm on screen.

- When the turtle is programmed to move forwards or backwards on screen, it may appear to children that the turtle is actually moving up or down. Unlike a floor robot, it will not always be possible for children to orientate themselves behind the turtle and so using Logo will require higher levels of spatial awareness.

- Children's experiences of using floor robots may produce unexpected results but may not prepare them for some of the screen turtle's behaviour. For example, programming the turtle to move forward 350 may cause the turtle to 'vanish' from the screen and pupils will need to understand why this has happened and how entering a further distance forward will bring the turtle back.

Working with primitives

It is important to introduce children to the correct syntax from the start and therefore worth teaching them the computer science principle Garbage in Garbage out [GIGO] and that when given errant commands Logo will process them but will return the message "I don't know how to …". Commands or procedures need to be typed into the command line at the bottom of the screen before being run.

It is worthwhile providing children with some primitives (basic commands) and emphasising the importance of adding a space between the command for turn or direction and the corresponding angle or distance. Like HTML, Logo commands are not case sensitive. Prompt cards help foster independence and can be tailored to the needs of the child or nature of the activity (see Table 5.1 below):

Table 5.1   Logo primitives

Instruction	Primitive	Instruction	Primitive	Instruction	Primitive
Forward	FD	Left	LT	Pen up	PU
Back	BK	Clear screen	CS	Hide turtle	HT
Right	RT	Pen down	PD	Show turtle	ST

Using primitives, children can experiment with drawing a house, a robot face, or writing their initials or name. These projects will provide challenge for pupils as well as plenty of opportunity for debugging as well as developing their sense of perseverance. Unfortunately, Logo does not have an easy undo command, and unless you use the editor to store commands as procedures Logo will not save your work.

Polygons and the turtle theorem

At this point, it is assumed that pupils will have created squares using Logo primitives. They may even be familiar with the repeat command from working with Roamer or Pro-Bot but need to understand the mathematics and use of brackets behind the code REPEAT 4[FD 100 RT 90]. The turtle theorem applies to any polygon they create and the rule is that the number of repeats multiplied by the angle of turn equals 360. Using this approach, they can use the theorem to create a circle REPEAT 360[FD 1 RT 1] and that by changing FD 1 to FD 2 they can increase the circle's size. Logo will also calculate the angle for any polygon for you by dividing the degree of turn by the number of sides e.g. REPEAT 4[FD 100 RT 360/4].

Storing procedures

The computing curriculum requires children to explain how algorithms work and introducing them to procedures provides an opportunity to model this. Procedures are stored using the editor (file menu, edit) and children should be encouraged to use sensible names with no spaces (choose 'save and exit' when done). So, creating a procedure for a pentagon, for example, can be modelled as follows (see Table 5.2):

Table 5.2 An explanation of an algorithm in Logo

Algorithm for Logo Procedure	Explanation of algorithm
to pent	To create a procedure for a pentagon (called 'pent') then …
repeat 5[fd 100 rt 360/5]	do the following things 5 times: Go forward 100 pixels and turn right 72° …
end	when done, stop the program.

Creating patterns

This introduces the programming concept of using one procedure to run another, for example, a procedure for a polygon to create a procedure for a pattern using that shape. To engage with this process, pupils will need to have created procedures for different polygons.

Begin by getting children to explore repeating a shape then adding an angle of turn each time. Pupils can be asked to predict and investigate the effects of changing the number of repeats and angle of turn. This invites prediction of what the pattern will look like and also reinforces the turtle theorem. In Figure 5.2 (below) a procedure for a circle called *circ* has been used to create two circle pattern procedures, cpat1 and cpat2.

Pupils can investigate the effects of changing variables, in this case, the number of repeats and the amount of turn.

A note about colour and the pen

A basic palette of 16 colours, each with a number from 1–16, are readily available, and pen colour can be changed in this way using the setpc command. For example, setpc 1 produces blue, setpc 2 green and so on. Changing the screen colour can likewise be achieved using the

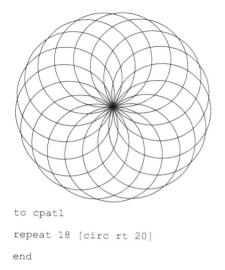

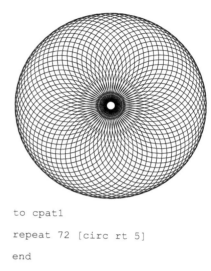

```
to cpat1
repeat 18 [circ rt 20]
end
```

```
to cpat1
repeat 72 [circ rt 5]
end
```

Figure 5.2 Using procedures to create patterns in Logo

setsc command. Pen thickness is changed by increasing pixel width using setpensize, so, for example, setpensize [3 3] will produce a thicker drawing line.

Activity: creating coloured patterns

Using what you have learned so far about Logo, try out the following activities:

1. Reproduce the Olympic emblem of 5 coloured interlocking circles as a one-word procedure.
2. Not forgetting the turtle theorem, use 3 procedures for three different coloured circles to create another procedure for a pattern (see Figure 5.2). The coloured circles should alternate in the same order each time.

Introducing variables

With Scratch, you may have added a variable, for example to record a player's score. By adding a data block this process is relatively simple and Scratch does the work for you. Adding a variable in Logo, however, requires writing the code and children will already have some experience of this from creating procedures for shapes and patterns. The easiest way to understand how variables work is to imagine that they are storage bins, into which you can place any number. The number is held inside the storage bin until the program wants it.

To demonstrate how this works in Logo, try creating a new procedure called 'shapes'. Add the following code, noting the absence of a space after the colon.

```
to shapes :length
cs
repeat 4 [fd :length rt 360/4]
end
```

Save this program and, from Logo's command line, enter the following: shapes 100

You will get a square on the screen – each side will be 100 pixels long. If you want to change the size of the square, simply run the program, but change the length. For example, running the command shapes 50 will result in the square's sides being 50 pixels rather than 100. Once you have one variable (in this case, length), you can add another – sides. Using this variable, you can decide the number of sides the shape will have. Edit the file, shapes, again, and change the code so that it reads like this:

```
to shapes :length :sides
cs
repeat :sides [fd :length rt 360/:sides]
end
```

In the command line, run the following script: shapes 100 6

This will result in a hexagon being drawn on the screen, with each side of a length 100. Explore the variables by changing the size for length and number of sides each time you run the program.

For loops

See the glossary for a definition, and the case study below for an example of using for loops in Logo.

Case study: meeting the needs of different learners

Kate is an NQT in a Year 6 class in a Junior school. Over the year, her mentor has been impressed with Kate's teaching of computing, and as part of a professional development session, Kate was invited to share practice with her peers on how she had used both text-based and block-based programs to teach the same programming concept to her class. Pupils in Kate's class had previously used Scratch in Year 5. The school operates a system of 'paired programming' (see Chapter 4) and, as you read the case study, you might want to think about the advantages this approach may have had in Kate's lesson.

Kate explained that as part of the Year 6 unit on Logo, the lesson objective was to understand how for loops work and to create them using colour as a variable in Logo. To do this, she

→

```
to anihex
wrap ht
pu lt 90
fd 500|
rt 90 pd
setpensize [5 5]
for [i 1 32 1] [
setpc :i
hex wait 10
penerase
hex pu rt 90 fd 20
lt 90 pd
penpaint
hex]
cs
st
end
```

Figure 5.3 Code for a 'for loop' in Logo

had introduced how to animate a shape to change its colour and move it across the screen. This involved using procedures the children had already made for shapes along with their knowledge of primitives. Kate then shared examples of the Logo programs that the children created (see Figure 5.3). She knew some children in her class would find this challenging and so decided to make the experience more concrete for them by using blocks in Scratch (see Figure 5.4). As Kate pointed out during the session:

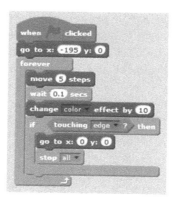

Figure 5.4 Using a loop in Scratch

The colour models and number of colours in both programs are essentially the same in that they use the RGB colour model, but they can be used to work differently in each program. In Logo there are 16 basic set pen colours which are each represented by a number. In Scratch colour can be chosen by mousing over a colour on screen or by increasing or decreasing the default colour value by a set amount using the looks block, which was something the children experimented with in their Scratch program.

Kate described how she also pitched the Logo work at an interim level for some of the children. Instead of using a "for loop", children used their existing procedure for a square (called "sq") and knowledge of primitives to write a procedure to animate their square (see Figure 5.5). Children used the wrap command (which allows the turtle to wrap around the screen when it gets to one edge) and the wait command.

Using programming partners Kate explained how each of the three activities themselves were able to be tailored depending on the pupils' level of understanding:

```
to movesq
ht setpensize [4 4]
wrap
repeat 4[
setpc 1 sq pu rt 90 fd 150 lt 90 pd wait 15
setpc 2 sq pu rt 90 fd 150 lt 90 pd wait 15
setpc 3 sq pu rt 90 fd 150 lt 90 pd wait 15
setpc 4 sq pu rt 90 fd 150 lt 90 pd wait 15
setpc 5 sq pu rt 90 fd 150 lt 90 pd wait 15
setpc 6 sq pu rt 90 fd 150 lt 90 pd wait 15
cs
wait 60]
st
end
```

Figure 5.5 Using 'repeat' to animate in Logo

*With the Scratch activity, not all of the children used the x y positions in their script or a control block to end their program. Instead, they physically moved the sprite or clicked the red stop button. Most created loops using the forever block with an **if... then** condition when it [the sprite] got to the edge, while some worked out the number of repetitions needed for the sprite to travel across the screen and used the repeat block. They were all able to explain and demonstrate how their program worked. The children working with "for loops" in Logo were encouraged to add an additional loop to change the screen colour. The activity to animate the square was also open ended in the sense that they could achieve the same result even if they didn't use the repeat command.*

You may wish to try out and tinker with the activities reported in this case study for yourself. **Note:** in Logo wait 60 = 1 second.

Kodu

Kodu (Microsoft, 2016) is a free Microsoft programming tool for children to make their own games **www.kodugamelab.com/**. Kodu uses sequences of numbered rows to create characters and in a similar way to the "**if … then** …" process in Scratch, Kodu uses the condition "when" *x* happens … then "do" *y*. Scripts are relatively simple to create and are constructed by selecting icons from menus so it neither truly uses either block code or script. The wonderful thing about Kodu, however, is that all the wizardry is there without you having to do very much – and desired outcomes are quickly achievable. For example, a simple program to control the Kodu character using the arrow keys yields immediate results with impressive 3D graphics. Compared to Scratch, there is no requirement to have any knowledge of coordinates or negative numbers in order to do this. There is, however, a need for spatial awareness, for example, when navigating characters or objects. Help with using the program is well supported with downloads, samples, lessons and starters as well as an online community forum.

As a gaming tool, Kodu naturally can be used to program game pads, and games can be swapped online using Xbox Live, but as such Kodu lends itself better to game design and teaching simulation rather than it does to the teaching of programming.

Python™

Python 3.5 (Python Software Foundation, 2016) is a professional script-based programming language which is more commonly associated with the teaching of computer science in Key Stages 3 and 4. However, it can be taught at basic level in upper Key Stage 2. The software can be downloaded for free **www.python.org/** along with a Python interpreter for ease of editing such as the Python 3 trinket **https://trinket.io/python**.

Some of the coding conventions in Python, such as the use of "if" and "else" may mirror programming concepts that pupils have encountered using IF statements in spreadsheets. In Scratch, this kind of **if … else** syntax is also familiar, and might translate into a script for a sprite and what to do when it encounters certain conditions. Prior work with Logo may also bring a degree of familiarity as Python is able to import and control a screen turtle. Switched on Computing (2016) provides a sound starting point from which to introduce Year 6 pupils to using Python (see further resources).

Activity: evaluating a programming tool

Select and access one of the programming titles listed in Table 5.3 below. Take time to evaluate and explore the tool, considering how you would use it as a teaching resource, and how pupils might engage with it. Having explored the tool, go on to complete a SWOT analysis (see Chapter 4, p.46). These questions will help you to consider the strengths, weaknesses, opportunities and possible threats of the tool.

Table 5.3 Programming tools for KS2

Title	Description	More information
Sherston Coding	Includes Scratch-based projects as well as adventure games to teach sensing and control	**http://corp.sherston.com/?page=sherston-coding** Free trial and download
Kodu	See above	**www.kodugamelab.com/** Free
Python	See above	**www.python.org/** Free
Raspberry Pi	Portable operating system which plugs into a TV or computer screen and provides educational resources for teaching coding	**www.raspberrypi.org/** See website for pricing, resources and downloads
VR Control	A 3D coding program to teach sensing and control	**http://camboardlearning.com/vrcontrol2.aspx** See website for demo and pricing

Research focus: pupils as digital leaders

Teaching pupils in Key Stage 2 how to *create, test, improve and refine sequences of instructions* through programming and using control technology has been a requirement of the national curriculum since 2000 (DfEE, 1999). However, although most teachers are confident in using technology to support pupils' learning, there has, historically, been a weakness in the teaching of control technology and programming (Ofsted, 2009; 2011). Even immediately prior to the introduction of the new computing curriculum there were, and most likely still are, many teachers who either lack basic IT skills or have significant gaps in their knowledge (Lin *et al.*, 2012; Morris and Burns, 2013; Prestridge, 2012).

Some teachers may feel threatened because they find themselves in situations where the pupil is more knowledgeable with technology than they are (Condie *et al.*, 2007; Ofsted, 2009). Seeking advice from pupils, however, should be encouraged because although pupils may possess digital skills which are in advance of their teachers' knowledge (Ng, 2012), it is possible for teachers to benefit by collaborating with younger people in order to develop their own computing skills (Helsper and Eynon, 2010; Teo, 2013).

There are schools which operate a system where pupils are selected as 'digital leaders' (Digital Leader Network [DLN], 2016). Typically, digital leaders might create school blogs, support teachers with using and planning with technology, or speak at Teachmeet sessions (Anderson, 2013). Where research evidence of digital leader activity in schools is reported, teachers have found that learning from pupils is not only highly useful, but 'inspirational' (Pachler *et al.*, 2010, p.73).

Activity: developing a programming community of practice

If you are teaching computing in Key Stage 2, you may find yourself learning along-side the pupils. Not just developing your knowledge of programming itself, but adapting to using a range of programming tools that may present the same content and concepts differently. Pupils may already have experience of the programs you are going to teach, and therefore building a community of shared knowledge and exper-tise has many benefits.

1. Begin by exploring the Digital Leaders Network website **www. digitalleadernetwork.co.uk/** and consider the ways in which this practice is relevant to teaching computing and how it operates in schools.
2. In your current school find out whether they have digital leaders or run a similar scheme which involves teacher-pupil collaboration using technology, and if they have, how it works.
3. If not, arrange to identify, meet and talk informally with pupils Find out what programs they are using, what they already know. Discuss with them what activities might appeal to the other children in the class and consider co-planning lessons with them.

Learning outcomes review

In the context of a school you know, respond to the questions or prompts which follow each of the intended learning outcomes as a means of identifying your knowledge and understanding of the content covered in the chapter:

- **Identify the Key Stage 2 curriculum requirements for programming.**
  Can you show evidence of lessons or activities that you have taught that address the computing PoS for Key Stage 2? For example, lesson plans, pupils' work, photographs?

- **Use and evaluate a range of software which builds upon children's skills knowledge and concepts of programming.**
  What are the key factors to be considered when choosing a programming tool for Key Stage 2 pupils?

(Continued)

(Continued)

- **Demonstrate your own knowledge of how to use different software programs to teach the computing curriculum at KS2.**
  Consider the ways in which you have acquired practical subject knowledge and evidence of this, e.g. through online tutorials, examples of resources or programs you have made to support your teaching.

- **Identify ways in which pupils and teachers can work together to support the development of programming in KS2.**
  Can you provide examples or illustrate how you have developed partnerships with pupils, for example, through knowledge exchange or co-planning lessons?

Further reading and resources

MSW Logo

A search on You Tube (**https://www.youtube.com/**) for 'MSW Logo tutorials' or "learn MSW Logo" will return a range of 'how to' videos (accessed 17 February 2017).

Glossaries of Logo commands

Available at:

http://derrel.net/ep/logo/logo_com.htm

www.steveharrell.com/computer/mslogocommands.html (both accessed 17 February 2017).

Scratch 2.0

The Scratch wiki provides a wealth of information.

Available at:

https://wiki.scratch.mit.edu/wiki/ (accessed 17 February 2017).

Phil Bagge's Code-it has a very useful section on the website which provides resources and advice on teaching game platforms with Scratch. Available at:

http://code-it.co.uk/scratch/primarygamesmaker/primarygamesmakeroverview (accessed 17 February 2017).

Python

Switched on Computing (Rising Stars, 2016) provides a sound starting point from which to develop work in text-based languages. Available at:

www.risingstars-uk.com/Series/Switched-On-Computing (accessed 17 February 2017).

6 Coding with HTML and Web Design

Learning outcomes

By the end of this chapter you will:

- have developed an understanding of the rationale for teaching children to code with HTML;
- understand the role of coding and web design in the primary computing curriculum and how these can be used to engage children at different stages of learning;
- know how to code with HTML yourself and identify how to teach this knowledge to children;
- identify potential opportunities to integrate coding and web design with learning across the curriculum.

Teachers' Standards

A teacher must:

2. Promote good progress and outcomes by pupils:

- be aware of pupils' capabilities and their prior knowledge, and plan teaching to build on these.

3. Demonstrate good subject and curriculum knowledge:

- have a secure knowledge of the relevant subject(s) and curriculum areas, foster and maintain pupils' interest in the subject, and address misunderstandings.

4. Plan and teach well-structured lessons:

- contribute to the design and provision of an engaging curriculum.

(DfE, 2011)

Introduction

Most web pages that you will come across are written in a language called HTML (Hypertext Markup Language). Although other scripts and codes may also be used, HTML provides the basic skeleton upon which the web page hangs. It is important at this stage to point out that HTML is not a programming language, but what is known in computing terms as a markup language. The concept of 'markup' originates from the traditional editorial process where paper manuscripts were annotated with written instructions for revisions, and so in this sense, HTML is a system for 'marking up' or identifying the components of a web page. This invariably involves things such as headings, paragraphs, pictures and lists as well as the features and attributes of these items such as font size, colour and alignment which determine how the web page looks in a browser. HTML is not immediately visible and lies behind the page you see, but knowing how to code with HTML basically allows you get 'under the bonnet' and control or change the way things look.

Activity: what's behind the page?

In your browser open a web page of your choice. Position the mouse to the side of the page (not on a picture or ad) and right click the mouse. From the options available, choose "View page source". This will reveal the **source code**, or the 'markup' of the page you were just looking at.

1. At the top, the first thing you should see is `<!DOCTYPE html>`. This is the Document Type Declaration (DTD) and it is important because it tells the browser the version of HTML that the page is written in. At the time of writing, this is HTML5.
2. You will notice how the doctype and some of the words in the code appear between chevrons `< >`. In HTML these are known as **tags**. From the source code you are looking at, see if you can find (use **ctrl F**), and note the `<title>` tag – which will give you the name of the page as it appears in the browser's tab.

The source code you have just looked at may well appear daunting, but this is because it also contains other elements such as JavaScript which many commercial websites use. Now try playing around with some code. Go to the X-Ray Goggles website **https://goggles.mozilla.org/**. Sign up for an account and then follow the instructions.

3. Try the mix and match activity 'What's my Name?' and watch what happens when you change the code.
4. Now, create a new tab and go to a website of your choice. Click on the X-Ray Goggles icon in your bookmark bar and then click on a head line or some text on the page. You should see an editor bar at the bottom of the page where you can change the text. Once done, click on update to see your new headline.

The above activities should give you a feel for the appearance of code and some experience of editing it which will help prepare you for the web pages that you will be creating in this chapter. **Note:** If doing this with children, stress that the actual web page will not change.

Before moving on to looking at why we teach children how to code with HTML, it is useful to consider and understand how the internet and the world wide web evolved.

Research focus: birth of the internet and the world wide web

In December 1999, *Time* magazine named Sir Tim Berners-Lee as one of the greatest minds of the twentieth century. In the wake of Gutenberg's printing press, Bell's telephone and Marconi's radio, his creation of the world wide web has similarly revolutionised society and the way we live in it.

Berners-Lee is self-effacing when it comes to his creation and admits much was down to the work of pioneers like Ted Nelson, who developed the concept of hypertext in 1965, and Douglas Englebart, who created the first computer mouse in 1968. By the late-1970s Vint Cerf, Bob Kahn and their colleagues had essentially developed the internet – the infrastructure which links computers together – and all that was left to be done with these components was to 'marry them together' (Berners-Lee, 2000, p.6).

In 1991, the world wide web went live and was made up of the three main components that Berners-Lee had invented: URLs – Uniform Resource Locators – which are unique identifiers for every web page; HTTP – Hyper Text Transfer Protocol – the means by which a web browser can communicate with an internet server using a language understood by each other, and HTML – Hyper Text Markup Language – the syntax used to encode web pages.

It is important to note that the internet and the world wide web are two different things. The internet is a vast communications infrastructure which connects computers together allowing them to communicate with each other. The world wide web acts like a skin that sits on top of this infrastructure and serves as the medium or way in which information is accessed over the internet.

Why teach children to code with HTML?

Aside from facilitating the delivery of the computing curriculum, there are a number of reasons why teaching children to code with HTML is a good idea.

(1) The resources needed to teach it are free.

(2) It provides a meaningful context and platform for children to develop their computational thinking.

(3) As a computer language, HTML is largely intuitive and easy to learn.

(4) Creating their own web pages is something most children find highly motivational.

(5) It is highly cross curricular and easily lends itself to differentiated learning.

(6) There are pedagogical arguments that the curriculum should not exclude the teaching of HTML (Csizmadia *et al.*, 2015) but that creative work with HTML should be an *explicit* requirement of the KS2 computing curriculum (Berry, 2013b).

The main focus of this chapter is concerned with teaching children HTML in upper Key Stage 2, although it is helpful to consider how progression in earlier age phases can help lay the foundation for this experience.

Developing web design concepts

EYFS

For most children in the Early Years, the internet will be pervasive and easily accessed through computers as well as mobile technologies. They may use the internet to read stories, explore concepts through games, or simply to find something out. If you are working with children of this age there are many opportunities for you to scaffold learning. Dialogue can easily be initiated by discussing the appearance, design and experience of navigating web pages: *The use of colour, pictures and sound; How easy is it to use? Do you know how to go to the next page or back to the home/start page?* In doing so, it is important for you to model and encourage the use of the associated language, for example: *browse, next, back, navigate, home, menu,* etc. Engaging the children in this way not only raises their awareness and experience of the internet as an end user, but also emphasises and encourages sequential thinking.

These experiences relate to the EYFS curriculum. For example, children are expected to know that information can be retrieved from computers and that they can operate some ICT equipment, know how to use it safely (BAECE, 2012) and can select it for a particular purpose (DfE, 2014). In doing so, children need to make the connection that clicking on different icons causes things to happen in a computer program (BAECE, 2012). This places emphasis on children this age being creative, inventive and developing their critical thinking by using *narrative and scientific modes of thought to develop and link concepts* and to *find meaning in sequence, cause and effect* (DfE, 2016, pp.20-21).

KS1

The development of programming skills, computational thinking and applications used to achieve these in Years 1 and 2 are covered elsewhere in this book (see Chapters 2, 3 and 4). In terms of developing their knowledge and understanding of web browsers, pupils in Year 2 can develop their skills by learning how to bookmark pages and use appropriate file management skills to retrieve them. They can also be shown how to use key words to find specific information on a web page by use 'ctrl F'. Developing their web search skills is also a good way to introduce them to hyperlinks to locate additional or related information (think Ted Nelson, here). In doing the above, they will be meeting the KS1 computing

PoS which requires them to *use technology purposefully to create, organise, store, manipulate and retrieve digital content* (DfE, 2013a, p.2).

KS2

Pupils in lower Key Stage 2 may already be familiar with creating their own presentations using PowerPoint or other multimedia tools. In terms of teaching one of the principles of how web pages behave, a good starting point is showing them how to hyperlink their slides.

Once some text or an image has been selected to act as the hyperlink it is straightforward in PowerPoint to set the hyperlink to go to another place in the document or to an external web page. Practical experience and knowledge of how hyperlinks function in one program and then learning to apply the principle when using HTML very much aligns with the computing 'purpose of study' in the national curriculum. Pupils are taught the principles of information and computation and how to put this knowledge to use when creating a range of content and in this sense children are developing their skills *at a level suitable for the future workplace and as active participants in a digital world* (DfE, 2013a). In light of this, it is worthwhile reminding ourselves that although a recent innovation the number of people across the globe with access to the internet continues to grow:

Research focus

The number of Internet users has increased from 738 million in 2000 to 3.2 billion in 2015*, according to a recent report from the International Telecommunication Union. That's a seven-fold increase that brought Internet penetration up from 7% to 43% of the global population (Jacob Davidson, *Time Magazine*, 2015).

In the United States, computer science jobs are growing at twice the national average; by 2020 there will be one million more computer science jobs than there are students who are studying the subject (Patterson, 2016).

* At the time of writing (April 2017) that figure is 3.6 billion and counting (**www.internetlive stats.com/internet-users/**).

Year 4 – 'We are HTML Editors'

This unit from the Rising Stars (2016) 'Switched on Computing' scheme of work is thorough and contains a lot of useful guidance. You may wish to look at how teaching ideas and activities are introduced and developed as much of it applies to this chapter.

Case study: switched on computing

As a new teacher, it is good practice to become acquainted with schemes of work that support the teaching of computing. In this case study, Dave Smith and Amanda Jackson give us an overview of how 'Switched on Computing' has developed, and how it operates in Havering schools:

In anticipation of the new computer science curriculum, we worked with Rising Stars and over a period of 18 months we contributed, developed and trialled the materials and resources with our Havering schools and Switched on Computing was launched in 2014.

One of the new things we developed was the unit on HTML. As part of the unit we felt it was important to build in an understanding of URLs and how the internet and the web works. There's a central program of training for teachers with phone and online support, and we also provide one-to-one support for teachers or year group teams in schools on anything they need help with.

Although teachers have found learning to code a challenge to begin with, they have been surprised at how quick the children are to adapt. The code does not faze them and pupils are quick to spot patterns and identify what they can tinker with. Ensuring they have the background knowledge and making it fun with things like X-Ray goggles are important.

Switched on Computing is currently used in over 6,000 schools in the UK, and its success can be gauged by the international levels of interest we've had in the scheme. We've just come back from rolling out the scheme in Qatar, and delegations from the ministries of education in Denmark and Japan have also recently visited, which is really exciting.

Many thanks to Dave Smith (computing and Online Safety Adviser and Business Development Lead) and Amanda Jackson (Inspector, computing and Online Safety and NQT Induction Coordinator), Havering School Improvement Services: hsis@havering.gov.uk www.havering educationservices.co.uk

If your school is using the Rising Stars scheme, then you will have access to all the materials. Otherwise, you can register as an individual:

www.risingstars-uk.com/Series/Switched-On-Computing

From the menu choose "Free Stuff" and filter your search by checking the "computing" box and then locate "Switched on Computing sample activities" from the results. You can then download the Unit 4.4 materials and resources including teachers' notes.

This chapter uses Notepad, an industry standard editor which can be found on most computers. Other HTML editors for children to use, for example Brackets (**http://brackets. io/**) can be downloaded. If you choose to do this in the school where you are, you must ask your mentor first. Alternatively, other online HTML editors such as Thimble are available but you need to sign up and create an account (**http://thimble.webmaker.org**).

Using Notepad to create web pages

This section is aimed at working with pupils in upper Key Stage 2. Before beginning there are several important points which you and the children need to know:

- ALL files relating to the web page(s) must be located in the same folder. If they are not, then pages will not load correctly.

- HTML uses American spellings which need to be observed e.g. 'color' not 'colour'.

- Filenames for all documents should not have any spaces in them and must include the extension e.g. ".jpg" etc.

- Everything needs to be spelled correctly and the code entered accurately including spaces.

- When pages load incorrectly, it is usually for one of the reasons above.

HTML can be typed in upper or lowercase although lowercase is recommended. Before beginning the tutorial below create a folder on your computer for your work e.g. **MyWebs**.

HTML5 Tutorial

There are many online tutorials but this chapter will use **W3schools**. There is minimal reading, it provides examples of code to play with, and most importantly explains how the tags work. Start with the introduction **www.w3schools.com/html/html_intro.asp** and work your way through each tutorial. When you get to "HTML Editors" save your work as instructed but save it to your 'MyWebs' folder which you created above and not your desktop.

A note about saving and previewing: You will have created one file called *Index.html* (or *Index.htm*). When you open it from your folder on your computer it is useful to view file **details** and check the file name **extensions** box:

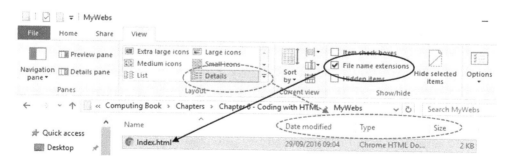

Figure 6.1 Screenshot previewing file details and extensions

As you work on your web page you will be opening the file in Notepad to edit it, and then your browser to view it. Each time you wish to preview your web page, you will need to refresh the page in the browser, or press **F5**. The routine is: Edit > Save > Preview > Edit > Save. To work between Notepad and your browser, you will need to use the "**Open with**" command. To do this, right click your *Index.html* file and select either program depending on what you want to do. If Notepad (or your text editor) or the browser you want to use is not listed then select "**Choose another app**" to find it.

During the tutorial, it is a good idea to experiment with the "Example" code by clicking "Try it Yourself" and then copying and saving it to your existing code into Notepad as you encounter it. When you are done with an example, close the tab to return to where you left off. Clicking on the "Home" button returns you to the main menu. To ensure you understand and can apply the code, the green box "Exercises" – which begin in the 'Attributes' Chapter – are worthwhile and could form part of pupil assessment.

Try working your way through the tutorial up to "HTML Quotations". You can skip the sections on "HTML Computercode" and "HTML Comments" as the content is not required at this stage. The next important tutorial to move on to is "HTML Colors".

Working with colours, Cascading Style Sheets (CSS) and links

You have already learned how to apply a limited range of colours to fonts and the background page. The "HTML colors" tutorial will introduce and explain to you the three colour models web pages use. The most versatile is the HEX (hexadecimal) Value which gives you 216 pigments each made up of a six-character code, so 'white' for example is '#FFFFFF' and 'black' '#000000'.

There are many sites which give you these colours, but the following one is particularly good because it allows you to see the colour you want and you can then copy the value into your code **http://tashian.com/htmlguide/websafe.html**.

If you are creating lots of pages, using stylesheets will save you time. You have already learned about **inline** styles to determine the appearance of things, such as fonts and colour, for example:

```
<h3 style="font-family:verdana;color:darkblue">This
is Heading 3</h3>
```

The W3schools tutorial also introduces using the **internal** method by using the <style> element in your web page which is coded directly into the <head> section of your page and you may wish to experiment with this. **External** style sheets involve creating a CSS file to contain this information which is then linked to in the <head> section of the web page. Developing the use of cascading style sheets is something which you may wish to introduce to extend your higher attaining pupils.

Developing knowledge of hyperlinks and working with images will be something all children will need to know. You will already have learned how to create a hyperlink to an external website and the "HTML Links" tutorial will show you the full scope of links. The most useful will be creating links to other web pages you make. The golden rule is that you should create the page before you make the link. For example, if your website is about the Romans and you want a link to a page on Roman food (roman_food.html), then the hyperlink in your *index.html* page might be as follows:

```
<p><a href="roman_food.html">Click here to find out
what the Romans ate</a></p>
```

Working with images

In the "HTML Attributes" tutorial you will have encountered and used the image source tag <img src=> to add a picture. The "HTML Images" chapter provides some useful guidance on working with images including the options for coding the width and height of pictures with pixels "width:110px;height:150px;" or by using the default setting you are used to: width="110" height="150". Using the CSS **float** property allows you to position an image to the left or right or centred within a paragraph of text. Although not included in the tutorial, you can add padding to one or more sides of your image to give it breathing space:

```
padding-top:20px;padding-right:20px;padding-bottom:
20px;padding-left:20px;
```

To add padding all round, the code would simply be: padding:20px

In the example code below, the image has padding to the right, and floats to the left:

```
<img src="any_pic.jpg"style="float:left;padding-
right:10px; width="110" height="150">
```

To align an image alone you can use the 'text-align' attribute that you have already used with text which aligns left, right or centre. The following code, for example, will centre the image on the page:

```
<p style="text-align:center;"><img src="any_pic.
jpg"></p>
```

The <center> tag is simpler and will do the same job and although not compliant with HTML5, it is supported by the main browsers:

```
<center><img src="any_old_pic.jpg"></center>
```

You will now have hopefully worked through all of the following "w3schools" HTML Chapters:

Activity

You should now have enough code and knowledge to create a meaningful and purposeful web page. Using your code, have a go at making an informative web page for your class which introduces coding with HTML in an attractive way. You may wish to refer to the example code (see below) and the associated web page (p.87) created using the tags that you have learned so far.

During the creation of your page you will be constantly **debugging** your code and will need to spend time refining it – a process you need to encourage in the children. Once you have created your own page, it will provide you with a model to share with the children.

Note: Web pages may well render themselves differently in different browsers so it is worth loading your work in different ones, e.g. Chrome, Safari, Microsoft Edge, Firefox.

```
<!DOCTYPE html>
<html lang="en-US">
<head>
<title>Chapter 6 "Coding with HTML"</title>
<meta charset="UTF-8">
</head>
<body style="background-color:lightcyan;">
<h1 style="font-family:verdana;color:goldenrod;font-size:250%;text-align:center;">Learning to Code With HTML</h1>
<hr>
<h2 style="font-family:verdana;color:darkblue">ABOUT THIS CHAPTER</h2>
<p style="font-family:verdana;font-size:110%;color:darkblue;" title=About This Chapter>
As a trainee teacher you are expected to be a proficient user of the internet both to support your teaching and your
wider professional role.<br>
<br>
This chapter assumes, however, that although you may already have a basic understanding of how the internet and web
pages work, you are not skilled in web authoring or creating web pages using code.<br>
<br>
In this chapter you will also learn about the pedagogy behind why it is important to teach children how to code.<br>
</p>
<h3 style="font-family:verdana;color:darkblue">MEET THE CHAPTER AUTHOR</h3>
<img src="dm_portrait.jpg" alt="David Morris" style="float:left;padding-right: 10px;width="110" height="150">
<p style="font-family:verdana;color:darkblue;"><br><b>David Morris</b> has over twenty years' experience in the
education sector. Before entering Initial Teacher Education [ITE] he worked in both the Primary and Secondary sectors
and has taught computing to children in every year group from Nursery through to Year 11.<br>
<br>
David has published educational texts on both student voice, and on the use of ICT and computing in secondary and
primary schools. He has published his research in peer reviewed journals and has delivered research papers at both
national and international conferences. David has previously written for Learning Matters' <i>Transforming Primary
QTS</i> series.<br></p>
<blockquote style="font-family:verdana;font-size:90%;color:darkblue;">
<br><h3 style="font-family:verdana;color:goldenrod">ABOUT SAGE AND LEARNING MATTERS</h3>
<i>SAGE was founded in 1965 by Sara Miller McCune to support the dissemination of high-quality research and teaching
content. <br>Today, we publish more than 850 journals, including those of more than 300 learned societies, more than
800 books a year,<br> and a growing range of library products including archives, data, case studies, reports, and
video. LEARNING MATTERS is an imprint of Sage.</i>
</blockquote>
<br><hr><br>
<center><img src= "Sage-lm.jpg" alt="https://uk.sagepub.com" width="332" height="65">
<p style="font-family:verdana;font-size:75%;color:darkblue;">
<b><i>Learning Matters, 1 Oliver's Yard, 55 City Road, London EC1Y 1SP</i> | Los Angeles | London | New Delhi |
Singapore | Washington DC |</b></center>
</p><br>
<a href="https://uk.sagepub.com/en-gb/eur/learning-matters" style="font-family:verdana;color:darkblue">Click here to
visit Learning Matters online</a>
</body>
</html>
```

Figure 6.2 HTML code for the web page on p.87

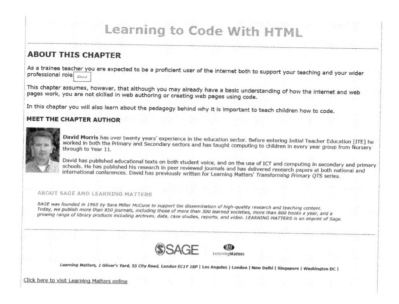

Figure 6.3 Web page for the HTML code on p.86. The hover message "About" only appears when you mouse-over the paragraph

Embedding videos, sound files and maps

Adding videos, music or maps to your web page is straightforward and looks impressive. The inline frame tag <iframe> allows you to embed content from another web page into your own. YouTube allows you to do this by selecting 'share' and then 'embed' which then gives you the code that can be copied:

Figure 6.4 Selecting HTML code for embedding video content

Other media sites like SoundCloud and Google Maps operate similar 'share, embed' processes.

Web design and layout

Developing children's skills and abilities with coding and debugging are important, but so is teaching them about the principles of good design. It is far easier for children to find fault with a poorly designed page than it is for them to identify why the design of a page is effective. Pupils may already have experience of evaluating designs, for example, peer-assessing each other's PowerPoint presentations, although when wanting to be critical of a piece of work, one good way of teaching this is to model a poor example you have created yourself.

Points to discuss with children should include choice of colours, font styles and sizes, use of illustrations, hierarchy of information, ease of readability, consideration of audience and general fitness for purpose. Although it is important how a web page looks, the prime consideration is not so much the appearance, but how it works (Robbins, 2012). Aesthetic choices concerning font colour and background are therefore secondary to the user's experience of how they interact with the user interface design. In his classic work on the principles of design, Norman (2013) identifies the two most important characteristics as being *discoverability* – what options are available to the user, and *understanding* – how to use the product. In this sense, and particularly if creating more than one page, it is a good idea for children to create a diagram or map of their web pages first in order to plan the structure – such as navigation – and content before creating them.

Making web design projects meaningful

The Rising Stars scheme that you looked at earlier provides suggestions for finding a theme or 'vehicle' for web design projects. This could be informed by the topic being studied, for example, online safety or work in another subject area such as the Romans. You need to find a focus which is purposeful and will motivate the children, as the following case study demonstrates.

Case study: 'The Band Project'

Jack and Jamilla completed their final teaching practice in a four-form entry primary school. Both were in a Year 6 class and both classes had just finished their SATs. They had six weeks left and their mentors asked them to plan a project that would keep the children motivated to learn. At their end of placement tutor group meeting, Jamilla and Jack were invited to share with the group why they felt their placement had been successful:

Jack: *Our university tutor came during SATs week so couldn't see us teach. We discussed planning instead and when we explained our situation she told us about the band project which she had seen work in another school before. She also mentioned, as an alternative, working on a charity project with the children.*

Jamilla: *We were lucky in a way because both projects our tutor suggested involved the children making websites, and our classes had done some work on coding HTML in Year 4 and so in the end our mentors thought it would be really good to build on that.*

→

Jack: *I decided to do the charity project with my class, and Jamilla, who sings in her spare time, was keen to do the band project.*

Jamilla: *The kids absolutely loved it and they really got a lot out of it. They came up with a band name and style of music and designed a logo for their band. They wrote fact files or bios and put together a world tour. They used GarageBand to record backing tracks and, as they created content, they were shown how to structure it into web pages. They also used the internet a lot. For planning the tour, they used an online interactive globe and real travel websites to calculate flight and hotel costs. They then used a spreadsheet to model the tour budget. They designed tour posters and album covers in Publisher, saved these as images and then added these to their websites. It was really cross-curricular and they were motivated the whole time.*

Jack: *Doing the charity project really meant a lot to my class. When they found out they were fund raising for a cause they could choose, they really got into it. They worked in groups and researched their chosen charity. They then wrote a persuasive bid as to why that charity needed their money more than others. They found out about the history of their charity, made flyers for their fundraising events and added this content to their website. They came up with some amazing ideas. For one week they organised different stalls and events in school. They used spreadsheets to record how much they raised and the school office wrote cheques that they then sent to their charity and the computing co-ordinator uploaded their pages onto the school website. It was an amazing experience and they gained a lot of confidence and pride in doing it.*

Activity: Web design projects

Reflecting on the case study, and using your medium-term planning as a starting point, discuss with your mentor how you might integrate the teaching of coding with HTML in a cross-curricular way using the following as prompts:

- Which themes or topics in other subjects might lend themselves? For example, an instructional website explaining a concept or process in maths or science for younger children to use; a website about a country studied in geography, or a biographical site on the life of a famous artist or historical figure.
- How will you engage and support pupils with EAL or SEN? Consider how approaches such as using templates or Word might engage children with the principles and concepts of coding.
- What are the implications for resourcing and access to the needed technologies? How will you organise the activities?

Understanding computer networks

The computing PoS Key Stage 2 (DfE, 2013a) requires children to be taught an understanding about how computer networks work. This is a complex and challenging area to teach (Berry, 2013b) and is beyond the remit of this book.

For those of you interested in developing your teaching of this area, a good place to start is with the CAS Quick Start Computing Toolkit (Berry, 2015) chapter on computer networks **http://primary.quickstartcomputing.org/computer_networks.html** which provides explanations, ideas, activities and links to resources. CAS Barefoot provide an unplugged lesson **http://barefootcas.org.uk/wp-content/uploads/2015/02/KS2-Network-Hunt-Activity-Barefoot-Computing.pdf** as a possible starting point for pupils. Camboard **www.camboard.com/windows.aspx** provide 3D educational software dedicated to teaching computer networks such as Inside the Internet or VR Server which simulates the main processes of a working server.

A final note

Before planning to teach children how to code and create web pages, it is worth noting the following:

- How will you support pupils who want to develop their work at home?
- How will you assess what children can do and what they need to do next?
- What opportunities are there for unplugged activities?
- How will you address issues of copyright on the internet?

Learning outcomes review

In the context of a school you know, respond to the questions or prompts which follow each of the intended learning outcomes as a means of identifying your knowledge and understanding of the content covered in the chapter:

- **Developed an understanding of the rationale for teaching children to code with HTML.**
  How has this influenced the way you plan learning experiences for children in the phase/year group where you were teaching? Provide examples from your practice to support how this has informed your practice.

(Continued)

(Continued)

- **Understand the role of coding and web design in the primary computing curriculum and how these can be used to engage children at different stages of learning.**
  What evidence do you have to demonstrate that you have been/would be able to differentiate the activities and learning experiences to meet and support the range of need in your class?

- **Know how to code with HTML yourself and identify how to teach this knowledge to children.**
  How does your planning, resourcing and/or lesson evaluations show that you are able to introduce concepts and knowledge in coding in manageable steps or sequences in a meaningful and relevant way with the children?

- **Identify potential opportunities to integrate coding and web design with learning across the curriculum.**
  What evidence do you have to demonstrate that you can teach children how to code web pages in different contexts or areas of the curriculum?

Further reading and resources

Mozilla Thimble

Online HTML editor plus starter activities. Requires registration. Available at:

https://thimble.mozilla.org

(accessed 17 February 2017).

W3Schools

A comprehensive tag list. Available at:

www.w3schools.com/tags/default.asp

(accessed 17 February 2017).

Code Academy

HTML tutorials – useful but lengthy instructions. Requires registration. Available at:
https://www.codecademy.com/ (accessed 17 February 2017).

Educator labs

Learning HTML basics with screenshots with a tag list. Available at:

www.teach-ict.com/programming/html/html_home.htm

(accessed 17 February 2017).

7 Using Computational Thinking and Coding to Create: App Building

Learning outcomes

By the end of this chapter you should be able to:

- identify what a mobile application (app) is and how they are used in various aspects of daily life;
- explain the difference between consuming and creating digital content;
- outline opportunities and ideas for children to create their own mobile applications;
- identify how computational thinking and coding can be developed through projects where children create mobile apps;
- evaluate and select appropriate app-building platforms for future classroom projects.

Teachers' Standards
A teacher must:

2. Promote good progress and outcomes by pupils:

- be aware of pupils' capabilities and their prior knowledge, and plan teaching to build on these.

3. Demonstrate good subject and curriculum knowledge:

- have a secure knowledge of the relevant subject(s) and curriculum areas, foster and maintain pupils' interest in the subject, and address misunderstandings;
- demonstrate a critical understanding of developments in the subject and curriculum areas, and promote the value of scholarship.

4. Plan and teach well-structured lessons:

- impart knowledge and develop understanding through effective use of lesson time;
- promote a love of learning and children's intellectual curiosity;
- contribute to the design and provision of an engaging curriculum within the relevant subject area(s).

(DfE, 2011)

Introduction

In recent years, technological advancements have led to continual improvements in the functionality of mobile devices. Smartphones have surpassed computers and laptops as the most common way of going online, and the increased range and simplicity of mobile applications allows users to carry out more and more tasks which only a few years ago would have required access to a computer (Office for Communications, 2015a). Mobile applications – commonly abbreviated as 'apps' – are software programs which are most commonly created to run on smartphones and tablet devices. Such devices come pre-installed with apps to meet the everyday needs of most users, for example, weather, news, photography, email, mapping and calculator apps. In addition to pre-installed apps, users can download additional (free or purchased) apps to meet the requirements for many other tasks. Additional apps are distributed via app stores, such as the Apple App Store, Google Play Store, Amazon App Store and Windows Phone Store depending on the mobile operating system used by the device. While apps are widely seen on mobile devices, their functionality is not restricted to such handsets, and apps can also be created for computers and ran over the internet, as can be seen with Google Drive which is an app which encompasses packaged software for creating and editing documents, spreadsheets and forms, etc.

Access and ownership of mobile devices among youngsters continues to grow, with approximately 40 per cent of children aged 5 to 15 owning a tablet computer or smartphone (Office for Communications, 2015b). This provides substantial opportunity for children to use a wide range of apps for both their education and entertainment. App development and distribution is a huge growth industry within the technology sector and can be used as stimulus in the classroom environment to develop children's computing and enterprise skills. This chapter looks at moving children from consumers of digital content to creators of apps and explores the potential of tools which can be utilised for app building in the classroom. It should be noted that there are many app building tools available online, many of which provide templates and 'what you see is what you get' interfaces to allow users to create apps with little or no coding required. While there is a place and purpose for such tools, the app builders mentioned in this chapter are those more commonly used in education, supplemented with tutorials and guidance for teachers.

Activity: apps in everyday life

In a short number of years, many of us have become reliant on the use of smartphones and apps in our everyday lives. Make a list of all the apps which you have used on your smartphone or tablet device in the past 24 hours. For each app, identify its

(Continued)

(Continued)

purpose, for example, productivity, travel, lifestyle, fitness, social, communication, etc. Consider how, without your smartphone or tablet device, you would have managed the task?

Now consider your school-based work environment. How could an app help you in your everyday life as a teacher?

App building and the computing curriculum

The building of apps may not be explicitly mentioned in the national curriculum for computing (DfE, 2013a), but there is huge potential for using app building to address the subject content requirements of all three curriculum areas – computer science, digital literacy and information technology. The app building tools discussed in this chapter are Key Stage 2 focused due to the level of programming expertise required, however, the exploration and use of apps will already be underway with children from a young age. As the use of tablet devices has grown in both home and school environments, children are increasingly well-versed in using a wide range of apps. This provides teaching and learning opportunities for Key Stage 1 (KS1) teachers to talk to pupils about the purpose of the app, its features as well as how the app can be used safely and responsibly. KS1 teaching can also begin to develop children's understanding of the design of the app through modelling, discussion and questioning, which explores the cause and effect of app buttons and links.

As children move into KS2, their prior programming experiences and computational thinking skills can be applied to app design and build projects. Without doubt, app building clearly meets the subject content requirements for computer science in KS2, as pupils will be required to *design, write and debug programs that accomplish specific goals* (DfE, 2013a), and in doing so they will be working with various programming features, such as inputs, outputs, variables, etc. In addition to the computer science learning opportunities, app building allows pupils to create digital content where online safety and responsibility have been considered. Before building apps, pupils will have explored and evaluated existing apps, where there will be opportunities to assess the design and usability of the app, as well as developing understanding of how and why advertising is used in digital content. When building apps, pupils will need to be aware of copyright issues in their selection of the images and sounds they may wish to use within their own apps.

Consumers to creators

While it can be assumed that children growing up today are digital natives, this does not necessarily mean that they are creators of content – instead it is most likely they are expert consumers of technology. Huba and McConnell (2012) coined the 1 per cent rule which was based on research into online communities, showing that just 1 per cent of users created the most content, 9 per cent interacted with content and the majority 90 per cent were described as lurkers – those who consume but never contribute. Huba's and McConnell's research dates back to 2006 and while the statistics may have changed, the general structure of online communities remains much the same. The need for more content creators and the importance of ensuring youngsters are equipped for the digital requirements of the workplace are strong themes within the computing curriculum.

The national curriculum for computing aims to provide an agenda which *equips pupils to use computational thinking and creativity to understand and change the world* (DfE, 2013a). This, along with the core of the curriculum which focuses on how digital systems work, encourages a shift from children being consumers to creators of digital content. The computing curriculum does not expect that all children will grow up to pursue careers in the technology sector, however, programming and computational thinking are important skills which encourage creativity, adaptability and innovation within an increasingly digital world. The ability to create is identified as one of the highest order thinking skills in Anderson *et al.'s* (2001) revision of Bloom's taxonomy, and in the digital-age, technology and programming affords significant opportunity for children to become creators (Caldwell and Bird, 2015). Both computational thinking and programming encourage children to explore, experiment and question ideas, especially where the chosen platform for programming provides an appropriate structure for children's creativity and ideas to be brought to life. App building not only provides children with the opportunity to create an app through a project-based approach, but they also get to publish and share their work to a wider audience both within and external to their own school community.

App building with AppShed

AppShed (AppShed Ltd., 2016) is an online tool for creating and publishing apps for Apple iOS or Android platform. AppShed allows users to tailor their approach used to app building based on their programming expertise. The tool is supplemented with the AppShed Academy, which provides comprehensive onscreen help guides, lesson plans, courses and video tutorials to support users through the app-building process. Having created apps, users can publish and share apps to the gallery, the web and app stores. AppShed provides a range of free and subscription-based account options including individual, business and education (EDU) accounts, with EDU accounts providing teachers with greater control to manage student accounts, progress and the moderation of pupils' apps before publishing.

AppShed makes app building achievable for different ages and programming abilities. Its interface provides a low-threshold, high-ceiling environment where users can start app building with a drag and drop interface, but can also view and interact with source code and programming languages.

Activity creating an app using AppShed

Start by visiting the AppShed Gallery (**http://appshed.com/appbuilder/academy/appsgallery**) where you can search and explore apps which others have created. You may prefer to search for apps which relate to specific topics of interest. You will notice that apps are shown in smartphone view to provide a 'what you see is what you get' environment. Exploring apps in the gallery will hopefully provide some inspiration for an app which you would like to create yourself.

- Before creating your own app, you will need to register for a free AppShed starter account by visiting: **https://appshed.com/about/getappshed**
- Once logged in, choose the 'AppBuilder' option.
- At the bottom of your screen you will see the AppShed Academy tab. Click on the arrow to pull up this tab and click on the 'Get Started Course'.
- This course lasts approximately one hour and will talk you through all the steps for creating your first app. As the AppShed Academy window remains at the bottom of the screen, you will be able to build your app alongside the step-by-step video and text-based guidance.

Project-based learning and computational thinking

App building lends itself well to a project-based learning approach. For children to create their own apps, there must be clear purpose and audience for the apps, and the best apps will be created where children have the time to develop and apply their knowledge, skills and understanding. Markham (2016) identifies the features of effective project-based learning to include the following components:

- start with a challenge, not a predetermined outcome;
- commit to inquiry;
- choose design projects which motivate children;
- use reflection and critical friends to analyse and fine tune projects;
- use visible thinking routines to accomplish specific goals.

Before teachers and pupils embark on app building, it must be recognised that such projects will span across a number of weeks, especially if an authentic project-based approach is to be utilised. Pupils will need to be given time to explore apps and how they work, before they can start designing their own. They will then need to learn how to use key features within the app-building tool before they can utilise the tool for their own project. The project will need ongoing opportunities for pupils to evaluate and refine their design and programming throughout the process, not just at the end.

Creating apps which address gaps in the market or provide solutions to specific problems also brings enterprise skills to the fore in children's learning, including collaboration, leadership, high expectations, staying positive (perseverance), problem-solving and creativity (Enabling Enterprise, 2015). There are many useful parallels between project-based approach and computational thinking. Many of the skills which children will develop and apply in app design and make projects will utilise the computational thinking processes and approaches discussed earlier in Chapter 2, such as logical reasoning, decomposition, abstraction, evaluation, debugging and understanding of algorithms.

When first designing apps, many children (and adults) may start with highly ambitious ideas which through decomposition will show the true scale and complexity of their intended creation. At this stage, unplugged paper-based planning will assist children in developing an understanding of how their app works and how different components link and behave. This will allow children to have an understanding of the components and algorithms they will need before being introduced to any tool for app building. As app building gets underway, teachers may find that the ambition of the original design impacts on perseverance levels and as such provides a good opportunity to show how programming projects will require ongoing evaluation, adaptation, debugging and perseverance.

Activity: understanding and planning for app design

Choose an app which you use regularly and know fairly well. When you first open this app, what types of components or buttons do you encounter? What type of content does each button link to? How do you get back to the app home screen?

Depending on the app which you have chosen, you may find that there are several links and buttons, therefore you may wish to restrict your exploration to just a few of the buttons and screens. Now have a go at drawing a plan for this app which shows components, screen page headings and links.

It is likely that your school already has a website, but it may not have an app. If you were going to create an app for your school, what content would you like users to have access to? Which buttons and links would be required? Would the links follow through to text-based content, documents, images, maps or video content? Create a plan for your app and you may wish to have a go at creating it using one of the app-building tools discussed in this chapter.

Apps for Good

Apps for Good is an organisation which promotes the use of technology in education to engage children and provide links to developers and experts who can help enable youngsters to research, innovate and build digital products which can potentially be taken to market. Apps for Good provide courses for upper KS2 pupils and beyond, which focus on all elements of app building, including both drag and drop and script-based tools. Expert guidance and mentoring is made available to participating schools via video conferencing, online training and in person during projects to provide support to both pupils and teachers. The Apps for Good program is built around an entrepreneurial approach where student teams are challenged to create their app from initial design through to marketing stages. Each year participating schools are invited to enter the Apps for Good Awards, which is a nation-wide event where school teams from around the United Kingdom compete to launch their app with the support of both Apps for Good and their sponsors in a Dragons' Den style competition. The apps which teams create all have a common purpose of improving lives in different areas, including: sustainability, accessibility, connecting communities, productivity and information-based apps. The following case study shows how one London-based school used the Apps for Good program as a stimulus for app building in upper KS2.

Case study: apps and social responsibility

Gearies Primary School is a three-form entry school in the London Borough of Redbridge. The school has a well-established history of effective use of technology for teaching, learning and engaging with the wider school community. Its commitment to technology as a positive agent for change has been recognised by the National Association of Advisors for Computers in Education (Naace, 2016) with a Third Millennium Learning Award and Gearies Primary is also a Naace Information Communication Technology Mark Accredited school.

Deputy Headteacher, Dan Lea and computing subject leader, Val Barker, have incorporated app building into their curriculum through providing pupils with clear context, purpose and audience for the apps they create. As a UNICEF Rights Respecting School (Drew, 2016), Dan explained the importance of children's opinions and ideas on social change and responsibility to be brought to the fore in their educational experiences. Having attended a training course on the use of the AppShed app-building platform, the computing subject leader, Val Barker, had introduced app building into the computing curriculum, supported through the use of linked units of work in the Rising Stars (2016) Switched on Computing Scheme.

Having discovered the Apps for Good program, both Dan and Val felt that the ethos behind the program, coupled with the AppShed platform and the Rising Stars scheme of work, provided teachers and pupils with the tools and framework for the building of apps with a focus on social change and responsibility. The Year 6 project was delivered through a

→

cross-curricular approach by class teachers, and enhanced through specialist teaching by Val, which took pupils beyond the drag-and-drop AppShed user interface and introduced them to more advanced programming skills within the platform, using the HTML source code. Val was able to track and plan for pupil progress using the Progression Pathways (Dorling and Browning, 2015) model.

In 2016, Year 6 pupils from Gearies Primary School reached the finals of the Apps for Good Awards with their Destination for You app. The app enables those with disabilities to plan journeys using London's transport system by providing accessibility information and tips. The app was spurred by pupils' anger when an individual was unable to travel with the school group using a London underground train line. Figure 7.1 below shows two screenshots from the Destination for You app, where pupils have identified destinations and linked to both audio and visual help guides they have created to assist users with their travel to specific destinations. As well as reaching the Apps for Good finals, the app also received attention and support from the local Member of Parliament.

Figure 7.1 Destination for You app created by Year 6 pupils at Gearies Primary School

MIT App Inventor 2

App Inventor 2 (Massachusetts Institute of Technology, 2015) is an open-source web tool used for creating apps for the Android operating system. Originally created by Google, it is now hosted by the Massachusetts Institute of Technology (MIT). As is the case for other MIT education tools, App Inventor allows users to create apps using a visual programming block-based interface similar to that of Scratch. App Inventor is supplemented by a wide range of tutorials and educational materials, links to which are provided at the end of this chapter. Before getting started with App Inventor, users will need a Google account to sign in, and to view app creations, they will need either an Android device or an Android emulator can be downloaded from: **http://appinventor.mit.edu/explore/ai2/setup-emulator.html**

Once logged into App Inventor, users start by creating the skeleton of their app in *Designer* mode. This stage consists of using the palette to drag-and-drop components into the viewer window which shows a smart device. Users can then go on to personalise each component in the properties window, for example, changing its name, background colour and font size as required. The user can then switch to the *Blocks* mode, where the behaviour of different components can be programmed. Figure 7.2 shows App Inventor in Designer mode where a user has created a random number generator app. In the *Components* pane it can be seen that the app consists of the following components which have been dragged-and-dropped into the viewer pane:

- Button 1 – The default button has been adapted by uploading a magician's hat and wand image. (It is important that children are aware of copyright issues and an appropriate image is sought, for example by filtering Google image searches according to the usage rights of the image.)

- Sound 1 – Sounds are non-visible components. In this case, a short copyright-free magic-themed sound file has been downloaded from the FreeSound website (**https://www. freesound.org**)

- Labels 1 and 2 – Provide text-based instructions for the app user.

Figure 7.2 MIT App Inventor 2 in Designer mode

If we now move to the *Blocks* mode (Figure 7.3), the programming for different components can be seen. In addition, the Android emulator is running enabling the programming results to be seen in smartphone view. The programming for each component is as follows:

- When users click on the button (magician's hat image) a random number between 3 and 99 will be generated.

- A sound (the uploaded sound file) will be played.

- A maths-based challenge will be randomly selected from a pre-programmed list of five challenges.

The program has been created by selecting each component and then using the Blocks pane on the left hand side of the screenshot. The viewer pane in the middle of the screen allows users to see their programming script, as well as copy-and-paste and delete blocks using the backpack and trashcan icons. The emulator on the right-hand side of the screen allows users to see how and if their app works, allowing for ongoing debugging and refinements to be made.

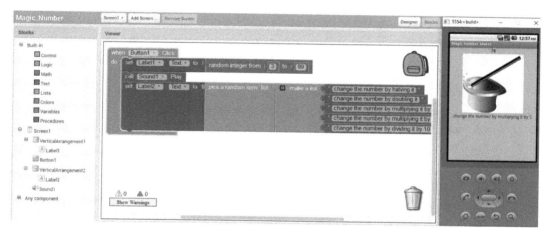

Figure 7.3 MIT App Inventor 2 in Blocks mode

If you would like to try App Inventor for yourself, follow this tutorial to create your first app:
http://appinventor.mit.edu/explore/ai2/hellopurr.html

Research focus: constructionism

Many of the visual programming languages explored in this book, and especially those founded by the Massachusetts Institute of Technology (MIT), have a secure foundation rooted in constructionist learning theories. Constructionism as coined by Seymour Papert, largely builds up Piaget's ideas on experiential learning and the philosophical theory of constructivism, where learning is a result of active, hands-on experience (Pound, 2006, pp.36–38). Papert defines constructionism as the construction of knowledge through building as opposed to transmission, coupled with the key idea that learners need to be engaged in the making of meaningful entities, *whether it's a sand castle on the beach or a theory of the universe* (Papert and Harel, 1991).

Papert deserves significant credit in bringing constructionism in the form of technology into the classroom environment. Programming languages such as Papert's Logo, Scratch, Star Logo TNG and LEGO WeDo all support constructionist learning approaches. App building tools such as MIT's App Inventor 2 also follow this tradition in providing children with the building blocks for their ideas within an environment where experimentation and tinkering are encouraged to create meaningful outcomes. In constructionism, the role of the teacher shifts away from a didactic, instructional style, to one where the teacher facilitates learning and mediates as required. When planning for computational thinking and programming, as a teacher you will need to carefully consider and evaluate your role in supporting pupil learning.

Case study: Year 6 app building project

During her school-based training placement, Katie, a trainee teacher, built apps with her Year 6 pupils. At the start of the placement, she was provided with medium-term plans for the half-term, which included planning for computing from the Rising Stars (2016) scheme of work for a unit titled We are App Planners.

As it was the summer term, Katie adapted the planning so that pupils' apps would focus on transition from primary to secondary school. The pupils had already started visiting their secondary schools as part of an orientation process, so Katie started by asking pupils for information which they felt would be useful for next year's cohort. Children's ideas included:

- How is secondary school different to primary school?
- Travel and journey guidance.
- Coping with homework.
- Making friends.
- Dealing with bullying.
- What equipment do I need?

→

- Uniform advice.

- Lunchtime advice.

- Top tips.

Katie split the class into groups of mixed-attainment pairs and children planned their apps using spider diagrams and smartphone templates. The class had prior experience in the use of visual programming languages in the form of Scratch, therefore Katie's mentor suggested that pupils created their apps using MIT App Inventor 2. This was not a program which Katie was familiar with, therefore she spent some time in familiarising herself with the app by following online tutorials and guidance in the Rising Stars scheme of work.

Katie introduced App Inventor to her pupils by modelling how to create a simple dice-rolling app, which the children then replicated and adapted in their own first app creations. Over the following four weeks, Katie's Year 6 pupils went on to create their own transition-themed apps. When evaluating the app-building project, Katie identified the following key strengths and areas for development:

Strengths:

- All pupils were able to insert buttons, change the title and upload a new button image.

- Most pupils understood the buttons and other components needed to be programmed for the app to work.

- Pupils identified similarities between programming of blocks in Scratch and App Inventor.

- Pairs supported each other well during programming and debugging.

Areas for development:

- The Android emulator did not work on school computers during the first lesson (Katie had tested this on her home computer). The school technician had to install the emulator ready for the next lesson.

- The apps which pairs had planned were far more ambitious than the apps which they created, as learning how to use the app was slower than expected.

- There were times when pupils wanted app features which Katie was unaware of and she directed pupils to stick to using the components which had been modelled.

Katie's last point suggests that she felt that children's exploration and creativity may have been restricted due to her own inexperience with the tool. How could she have encouraged children to explore the use of different components in a structured and purposeful manner?

Learning outcomes review

This chapter has explored how designing and building apps can develop children's computational thinking and programming skills through providing a meaningful context for children to utilise their ideas. In the context of a school you know, reflect on the questions below in relation to each learning outcome from this chapter.

- **Identify what a mobile application (app) is and how they are used in various aspects of daily life.**
  Identify which apps are popular with your pupils and together categorise them according to their purpose.

- **Explain the difference between consuming and creating digital content.**
  Evaluate the computing content which you have planned and delivered this year. Have you provided opportunities for children to create and share content?

- **Outline opportunities and ideas for children to create their own mobile applications.**
  Analyse your subject-based schemes of work to identify opportunities where app building can be used in a cross-curricular approach with another topic area.

- **Evaluate and select appropriate app-building platforms for future classroom projects.**
  Explore one of the app-building tools mentioned in this chapter. What are the benefits and limitations of this tool?

- **Identify how computational thinking and coding can be developed through projects where children create mobile apps.**
  While exploring the app-building tool of your choice, identify which computational thinking processes and skills you are using. (See Chapter 2 for a list of computational thinking skills and processes).

Further reading and resources

Apps for Primary Schools

Available at: **www.apps4primaryschools.co.uk/** (accessed 17 February 2017).

While not specifically linked to app building, this is a useful site for any teachers or schools who have invested in tablet devices and wish to explore which educational apps are available. Searches for apps can be filtered by platform, key stage and subject.

Apps for Good

Available at: **https://www.appsforgood.org** (accessed 17 February 2017).

Apps for Good is an organisation which links teachers in schools and to industry expert volunteers with the aim of creating apps which have appositive impact. The course content and annual competition is open to pupils between the ages of 10–18.

AppShed

Available at: **https://appshed.com/** (accessed 17 February 2017).

AppShed is a free and subscription-based online app-creation tool allowing users to design and publish mobile apps for iOS, Android and web. AppShed users can engage with app building through a variety of approaches including a drag-and-drop interface, source code and programming languages. AppShed Academy provides educators with additional tools, resources and support materials to aid teaching and learning.

Blippit IO

Available at: **https://www.blippit.co.uk/** (accessed 17 February 2017).

Blippit IO is a suite of computing tools for KS2 and KS3, which includes an app builder tool. Blippit IO provides various free and subscription-based options for schools, including access to an extensive knowledge base and Blippit Academy for teachers. It should be noted that the app builder tool requires access to the Google Chrome browser and a user account needs to be created.

MIT App Inventor 2

Available at: **http://ai2.appinventor.mit.edu/** (accessed 17 February 2017).

MIT App Inventor 2 is an open-source web tool used for creating apps for the Android operating system. A Google login is required and getting started guidance can be found here: **http://appinventor.mit.edu/explore/beginner-tutorials-short.html** (accessed 17 February 2017).

TouchDevelop

Available at:

https://www.touchdevelop.com/ (accessed 17 February 2017).

TouchDevelop has been created by Microsoft and provides an online visual programming environment where users can create apps for tablets, smartphones and computers. It provides a cross-platform environment which enables users to view apps on different operating systems. TouchDevelop provides online tutorials and guidance for those who are new to the tool: **https://www.touchdevelop.com/docs/getting-started** (accessed 17 February 2017).

Websites for Copyright-free images and sounds

Creative Commons

https://creativecommons.org/ (accessed 17 February 2017).

Google 'free to use' Image Search Guidance

Guidance for Google image searches - https://support.google.com/websearch/answer/29508?hl=en (accessed 17 February 2017).

FreeSound

Available at: https://freesound.org/help/about/ (accessed 17 February 2017).

8 Using Computational Thinking and Coding in Gaming

Learning outcomes:

By the end of this chapter, you will:

- be familiar with the digital native/digital immigrant debate and how this could inform your lesson planning in computing;
- consider how computational thinking is relevant in games design and how you could implement this in your teaching;
- identify with some current software platforms that can be used to deliver coding lessons through game creation;
- review the use of gamification pedagogy and its links to thinking computationally.

Teachers' Standards:
A teacher must:

2. Promote good progress and outcomes by pupils:

- plan teaching to build on pupils' capabilities and prior knowledge;
- demonstrate knowledge and understanding of how pupils learn and how this impacts on teaching;
- encourage pupils to take a responsible and conscientious attitude to their own work and study.

3. Demonstrate good subject and curriculum knowledge:

- have a secure knowledge of the relevant subject(s) and curriculum areas, foster and maintain pupils' interest in the subject, and address misunderstandings.

4. Plan and teach well-structured lessons:

- promote a love of learning and children's intellectual curiosity;
- reflect systematically on the effectiveness of lessons and approaches to teaching;
- contribute to the design and provision of an engaging curriculum within the relevant subject area(s).

(Continued)

(Continued)

5. Adapt teaching to respond to the strengths and needs of all pupils:

- have a secure understanding of how a range of factors can inhibit pupils' ability to learn, and how best to overcome these;
- have a clear understanding of the needs of all pupils, and be able to use and evaluate distinctive teaching approaches to engage and support them.

(DfE, 2011)

Introduction

This chapter will discuss how teaching computing and computational thinking can be enhanced by adopting a 'game-based' context. The use of games in supporting learning is historically embedded in education and our schools. Ancient Roman culture, for example, saw the *ludus* governed by a *ludi magister* (school teacher). *Ludus* (plural *ludi*) can be interpreted as 'game', 'board game' or 'play'. Primary school teacher colleagues are well versed in the pedagogy of using play and games to enrich the learning of their children. Therefore, positioning computing education within the context of game design will be supportive of existing experience and expertise of those tasked with the challenge of delivering the primary phase curriculum.

With this in mind, it is also important to situate learning in contexts that our children 'get'. Prensky (2001) presents the digital native/digital immigrant contention. A digital native has been born into and brought up in the digital age making them confident 'native speakers' of technology and technological devices. Digital immigrants were born before the age of digitisation (Prensky uses 1980 as an arbitrary date) and as such are not as familiar or immersed in the language of digital technologies. We could now unlock this digital native debate and deliberate whether our young people are indeed 'digital natives'. For example, what about the digital divide? Those who 'have' and do not 'have'? Just because I speak the 'language' does it mean I understand what I am saying? Does confidence in technology equate to competence? However, the argument is that a teacher should plan lessons that meets the needs of their pupils. Our children live in a digital world. They are immersed in technology from a very early age and by the age of 21 our children are likely to have spent 10,000 hours playing video games (McGonigal, 2012). It is estimated that 99 per cent (5.9 million) 8–15 year olds in the United Kingdom play games (IAB, 2014). Teachers should plan creative lessons that promote a love of learning and that will lead to high-quality progress and outcomes. Placing aspects of Key Stage 1 and 2 computing scholarship in a 'game-based' pedagogical context will support this and allow the pupils to embrace their learning from a standpoint they recognise, are engaged by, understand and 'get'. Using a game design context will help reduce the complexity of learning computer science by placing learning in a fun and engaging context and ensuring the correct levels of motivation and 'creation' needed for progress.

Activity: time to reflect

Are you a digital native or immigrant? Is this important? Where do you position yourself in using game-based contexts as a tool for learning? Are you a game player? Most of us are to some extent (65 per cent of 16–74 year olds or 27.6 million adults in the UK play games (IAB, 2014)) – think mobile phone apps, for example.

As you begin to develop your teacher identity, what are your initial thoughts in embedding gaming as a pedagogy and/or a learning context in the computing lessons you are developing?

What is computational thinking and how does it fit with gaming?

Computational thinking was discussed in detail in Chapter 2. However, in embracing the concept that learning does not have to be linear, you may be reading these chapters using a more randomised approach. With this in mind, let us recap what computational thinking is.

Computational thinking is a term coined by the computer scientist Jeanette Wing in 2006. Wing describes it as a skill as vital in the twenty-first century as reading, writing and arithmetic understanding. Computational thinking is not necessarily about computers and computing. It is about 'real world' problem solving and how we go about understanding a 'problem' and develop the solutions to solve it, using logical thinking. Something as simple as coming to the end of my supermarket shopping – and having to solve the problem of which till may have the shortest queue, or the till with the most efficient sales assistant, or which queue has the customers with the least amount of items in their baskets – could all be described as thinking computationally.

There are six procedures or techniques required in computational thinking.

Logical thinking: underpins the way you think computationally and are able to choose the best solution for the 'problem' being considered.

Decomposition: how a difficult problem can be 'broken down' into something that is easier to understand.

Pattern recognition: are there any similarities between the different parts of the problem? Or are there similarities between the parts of this problem with that of another problem's solution?

Abstraction: removing and ignoring the details that are not needed and concentrating only on those details considered relevant to solving the problem.

Algorithm creation: once the problem is solved it can be written up in a set of logical steps.

Evaluation: an ongoing approach to checking that the solution being created meets the requirements of the 'problem'.

Once the algorithm is created then the following procedure could be implemented:

Automation: turning the algorithm into a program that a computer can execute.

Computational thinking is, therefore, scientific in its underpinnings, but essentially also requires the solving of problems efficiently from a creative, innovative and critical position.

Activity

Can you begin to think of the benefits of thinking computationally and how computational thinking may be applied to games design?

Why should computational thinking encourage creativity and innovation?

From a digital games perspective, innovation and creativity are obvious facets that need to be embraced by those involved in the industry – and also by pupils looking to create and code a game as part of their computing curriculum experience. Digital game design and creation is an excellent medium to use in underpinning computational thinking and understanding, as well as developing innovative and creative thinking. It is also a recognised and well-researched method for introducing and delivering programming and coding concepts (e.g. Smith and Grant, 2000; Leutenegger and Edgington, 2007; Al-Bow *et al.,* 2009; Kazimoglu *et al.,* 2012). As suggested earlier in this chapter, children will be familiar with the features of digital video games. They play them on their computers, consoles, televisions, tablets and mobile devices. Children are, therefore, likely to be enthused by this context and be challenged by the creativity and innovation of the various solutions they could develop in creating their game.

Consider the following case study as an example of how you might embed computational thinking within the context of your pupils developing and coding a digital game.

Case study: game design and computational thinking

This case study is drawn from a scheme of work created by a Primary with computing trainee teacher (Harry) for a group of Year 5 mixed-ability pupils. The pupils are asked to be video game designers tasked with designing a simple game using the *Scratch* platform. Harry's intention is to underpin the Scratch game-design learning using the cornerstones of computational thinking, as well as to introduce some basic programming concepts. Throughout the series of lessons, Harry emphasises the need for his pupils

$\longrightarrow$

to make mistakes in supporting ways of thinking computationally. For example, making mistakes will help develop the confidence in dealing with complexity and the pupil's persistence in working with difficult problems. Harry wants his pupils to be independent in achieving goals that they set for themselves. The case study highlights experiences drawn from Harry's reflections on planning and delivering his lessons.

Harry acknowledges the importance of his pupils not immediately accessing Scratch and 'doing' the game if computation principals are to be followed. Ensuring his pupils participated in the creative processes needed to 'create' was vital. One of the first things Harry asks his pupils to do is to simply play a 'game' with a view to recognising the 'rules' involved. From a computational thinking perspective, identifying and 'breaking down' the rules to a game is helping to underpin the notion of pattern recognition and decomposition and already developing the learning required here. It also provided an immediate opportunity to introduce the familiar fun and engaging aspects the children would benefit from.

Depending on the complexity of the game provided (in this case it was a modelled Scratch game that Harry had developed himself) you could go further and ask your pupils to consider how the game works and the instructions needed within the game. This approach would start to encompass early algorithmic thinking and design with your pupils.

Harry decided to create his scheme of work using some aspects of a typical 'software development life cycle (SDLC)' and thus create some 'real' foundations to the learning journey for his pupils, whilst also trying to ensure the 'pitch' was right for his pupils. There are generally six stages to a SDLC (depending on the method used). If adopting a traditional Waterfall method, the below stages are typical:

1. Investigation

2. Analysis

3. Design

4. Development

5. Implementation

6. Operation and maintenance

1. During the *investigation* stage, Harry asked his pupils to identify and define the *'problem'*. This involves deciding the game the pupils wish to create, why they wish to create it and whether it is feasible to do so (based on their expertise, the scope of the game and the limitations of Scratch as a platform). The pupils were also asked to 'fact find' and develop a short questionnaire that allowed them to see if their game ideas were welcomed. The pupils were expected to document their proposal via a writing frame that Harry provided.

$\longrightarrow$

2. The *analysis* stage allows the pupils to *decompose* the *problem* and start to detail the game proposal, rules and solution. *Abstraction* and *pattern recognition* is also applied here in asking the pupils to consider only the features of the game that were essential and encouraging them to think what patterns or rules to the game could be repeated or replicated. Harry decided to introduce *flow charts* (using appropriate flow chart symbols) as a way of visually representing the pupils' proposed solutions. This also allowed *algorithm* understanding to be introduced.

3. *Design, development and implementation* stages converts the proposed solution from the previous stage into a series of design specifications to meet the end user need before developing the game in the chosen platform. Harry decided to develop the flow chart idea and introduce some simple *pseudo code*. This allowed for further expansion of *algorithmic* understanding as well as enhanced exploration of *decomposition, pattern recognition and abstraction*. Pictorial representation of the game was also developed as well as the 'jigsawing' of Scratch code using laminated paper copies of Scratch 'procedures' that Harry had produced. During these stages, the game is created and coded in Scratch. Pupils were asked to keep a coding diary and comment on the code used and what their game is doing as it is created.

4. *Testing and debugging* took place with the pupils self-reviewing their work. Harry also introduced peer review as a pedagogy and paired his pupils up at various points throughout the project to test their peer's game and offer feedback on how to improve it. Harry sometimes allowed this to be completed informally. However, he also introduced a formal testing and review point where he used a worksheet he had designed to ensure the pupils were targeting the correct aspects of their game's programs during their reviews.

5. *User documentation* and game play instructions were created by the pupils and tested by their peers. This provides a further opportunity for the pupils to articulate their approach and develop their understanding of the computational and coding choices they have made.

6. *Evaluating and reflecting*. Harry decided to do this via a presentation that the pupils gave (which he also filmed as a means of evidencing the understanding and progress shown). Pupils were asked to:

   - present their plans and flow diagrams outlining the initial ideas and algorithm proposals;

   - present their game solution, understanding and the user/game-play instructions;

   - discuss the choices they made – how they broke down the problem and removed what was needed;

   - evidence how they tested and improved their game based on the tests and reviews conducted.

→

Teacher reflection

In his reflection, Harry was happy with his approach to the learning. Most pupils developed their game with confidence and by ensuring that a loosely followed SDLC approach to the learning took place, they also engaged with other aspects of software development. His approach ensured key programming terminology and concepts were tackled and not just those associated with Scratch. Harry found that he did have to explicitly keep referring to the computational thinking procedures taking place and where, to ensure the pupils were developing their capability in these areas. This repetition aided the pupils' learning and understanding of the fundamentals he wanted to underpin the work.

Table 8.1 Game design and computational thinking

Case Study 1 Summary:			
Computational thinking technique?	**Activity/Task?**	**Outcome?**	***KS2 national curriculum link?***
Problem recognition	What digital game are you creating? Why? Is it feasible?	— Fact finding survey. — A brief explanation of the game idea and why/how the pupil considers it feasible to develop.	
Decomposition	Recognising and mind-mapping rules of existing games as well as the proposed game. Developing a plan to complete the game.	— Existing game(s) rules — Proposed game rules and levels — Action plan?	
Pattern recognition	Spotting replication and using programmable functions to create repeatable patterns in the game.	— Programmable procedures/ functions incorporated into the Scratch game eg. Loop, repeat.	— *use sequence, selection and repetition in programs; work with variables and various forms of input and output*
Abstraction	Selecting only details and features applicable to creating the game. Discarding anything deemed irrelevant.		
Algorithm design	Create a flow chart(s) to model the proposed game solution that demonstrates an algorithm designed to complete the game.	— Flow charts — Pseudo code? — Scratch game development	— *use sequence, selection and repetition in programs; work with variables and various forms of input and output*

(Continued)

Table 8.1 (Continued)

Case Study 1 Summary:			
Computational thinking technique?	Activity/Task?	Outcome?	*KS2 national curriculum link?*
		– Programmable procedures/ functions incorporated eg. Loop, repeat. – Knowledge of inputs, processes and outputs demonstrated.	*– use logical reasoning to explain how some simple algorithms work and to detect and correct errors in algorithms and programs.*
Logical thinking	Used throughout project in developing the solution for the game proposal.	– game rules and instructions. – user documentation. – video evaluation output displaying the pupil's thinking behind their work.	*– use logical reasoning to explain how some simple algorithms work and to detect and correct errors in algorithms and programs.*
Automation	Using Scratch to create the proposed game solution.	– A workable Scratch game.	*– design, write and debug programs that accomplish specific goals, including controlling or simulating physical systems; solve problems by decomposing them into smaller parts* *– select, use and combine a variety of software (including internet services) on a range of digital devices to design and create a range of programs, systems and content that accomplish given goals, including collecting, analysing, evaluating and presenting data and information*

What is important is that the learning provided by designing and programming a digital game is underpinned at all stages by the concepts of computational thinking. The learning of programming concepts, constructs and fundamentals should be reinforced where possible. It is not just about 'doing' something in Scratch (for example) or the excitement of creating a game. The teacher needs to plan for and create lessons that develops and progresses pupils' capability with both programming and computational thinking.

Tools for creating digital games

There are many widely available tools and software available for primary school pupils to automate, program and code a digital game. Accompanying these tools is a plethora of online and written material for learning and using in the classroom. The following software is often used in schools as a means of introducing and developing programming and coding from a game design context.

Scratch

Scratch (available at: **www.scratch.mit.edu**) is a free tool that allows you to program your own interactive stories, games, and animation (MIT, 2016b). It utilises coding and programming concepts, but does so using graphical 'blocks' that the user can 'jigsaw' together to create the program they are developing.

Kodu

Kodu is a Microsoft developed integrated programming environment (available at: **www.kodugamelab.com/**). It is designed for children to create games and learn how to programme. As with Scratch, it does not require the typing of code but uses a game controller to embed visual components in creating the 'game'.

GameMaker Studio

This software environment (available at: **www.yoyogames.com/gamemaker**) uses a 'drag and drop' approach to creating the programme. It utilises a programming environment but again, without the need for the pupils to engage with the complexity of writing the actual code. The tool allows the creator to export their games to a variety of platforms.

Alice

Alice (available at: **www.alice.org/index.php**) is a 3D programming environment. It also uses a 'drag and drop' approach to creating a programme. Alice is designed as an introductory tool for programming, but will allow pupils to engage with all programming concepts and constructs.

GameSalad

Game Salad (available at: **http://gamesalad.com/**) is designed to teach computer science and programming through the medium of game design. It too dispenses with the need to code and uses the familiar graphical 'drag and drop' approach.

Tynker

Tynker (available at: **https://www.tynker.com**) is another creative tool designed to teach children how to program and build games and mobile applications. Lesson plans, tutorials and assessment guidance are provided.

All the above software options (and others you may find online) will allow for the development of computational thinking and programming concepts. They are designed to be accessible by children of all ages. They are also clearly focused in achieving and progressing the pupils within the computing programme of study at Key Stage 1 and 2 (DfE, 2013a). The below descriptors, taken from the 2014 national curriculum for computing, will be achievable using the software applications identified in this section.

KS1

— understand what algorithms are; how they are implemented as programs on digital devices; and that programs execute by following precise and unambiguous instructions;

— create and debug simple programs;

— use logical reasoning to predict the behaviour of simple programs.

KS2

— design, write and debug programs that accomplish specific goals, including controlling or simulating physical systems; solve problems by decomposing them into smaller parts;

— use sequence, selection and repetition in programs; work with variables and various forms of input and output;

— use logical reasoning to explain how some simple algorithms work and to detect and correct errors in algorithms and programs.

(DfE, 2013a)

Activity: resource evaluation

1. Explore the software applications listed earlier and start to consider which one will work best for you and the pupils you are about to teach.
2. Make a list of the different features they each offer and the complexities that may be faced in using them as tools to develop a coded game.
3. Consider how computational thinking could be used to support and underpin the learning and game development within the software.
4. Which one might you choose to use? Why?

What about gamification?

Gamification is a relatively new pedagogical concept beginning to permeate education. Gamification has been described as the use of game design elements in a non-gaming context (Deterding *et al.*, 2011). It is not creating and coding a game. Rather, it is an approach that encourages intrinsic motivation by using game mechanics (the game rules and actions), dynamics (how the game 'plays'), aesthetics (the experiences felt in playing the game), and game-based thinking in promoting learning and problem solving (Kapp, 2012). Gamification extracts the elements that make digital games fun, addictive and exciting to play and embeds them in the teaching and learning journeys being developed for pupils. This could include the use of badges, points, trophies, rewards, goals, levels, timers, leaderboards, characterisation, alternate pathways/storylines and anything else that encompasses a 'game'. Technology is not necessarily required and an 'unplugged' approach may be adopted, but the problem-solving aspect of gamification represents a tangible link with the skill of thinking computationally. Gamification also sits comfortably within the contexts our twenty-first century learners are familiar with by using game ideas and approaches that young people will recognise, accept and choose to play because it is fun. Gamification pedagogy and techniques therefore aim to impact positively on motivation and pupil progress – and avoid the difficulties of being able to identify with, access and engage with the taught curriculum. If planned for thoroughly, gamification strategies can be significant in engaging your pupils and increasing their adherence and completion of activities.

Research focus: flow theory and self-determination theory

The pedagogy of gamification is supported by the theories of *self-determination* (Ryan and Deci, 2002) and *'flow'* (Csikszentmihalyi, 1990). *Self-determination* theory explores the conditions that need to be in place for people to be self-motivated in their personality, behavioural development and the work they are conducting. *Flow* refers to intrinsic motivation that can be symbolised by a person being completely absorbed in what they are engaged with and undertaking. Gamified approaches seek to enhance players' (pupils) engagement and involvement by adopting these intrinsic characteristics to motivation. It can be argued that gamification and gamified approaches to learning will therefore stimulate this state of 'flow' (McGonigal, 2011; Miller, 2013) and will engross the pupil in learning that is engaging, creative, challenging and capable of resulting in high performance (McGonigal, 2011).

Huang and Soman (2013) suggest the concept of gamification is simple, but applying gamified methods to teach a concept effectively is not so simple. They recommend a five-step approach for streamlining the process.

Drawing on the learning earlier in this chapter, the links to computational thinking are clear. **Steps 1** and **2** are entwined with identifying the *problem* that exists. These steps also require *decomposition* and *abstraction* in identifying only what is relevant in solving the problem and setting appropriate learning objectives. *Decomposition* and *pattern recognition* will be required in completing **Step 3** and **4**. This will ensure the learning experience is properly broken down into manageable 'chunks' and whether gamified techniques used in a different part of the curriculum might be appropriate. **Step 5** equates to the *algorithm* and the creation of the solution in completing the activities set for the pupils.

It may well be that creating a digital game is not a viable option. The resource may not be available; perhaps you do not feel confident enough in using the technology; or maybe there is not time in an already crowded curriculum to get the pupils to create the game on computers. Adopting a gamification approach to develop computational thinking skills and capabilities, and progressing some game design understanding, could be an alternative or further option alongside that of developing a game.

Case study: gamification

This case study explores the concepts of gamification and computational thinking with a Year 6 class. Sarah learned about gamification pedagogies during her initial teacher training and was keen to embed it in her teaching. Sarah used the ideas of gamification to plan and deliver a short sequence of lessons designed to teach computational thinking and programming through designing a game in the Kodu platform. Drawing on Huang and Soman's research, her initial approach had her pupils defining the game design 'problem' presented to them. They were also asked to justify the objectives of their solution and detail the requirements they thought they would need to meet in their game. In other words, a project plan was created. This also allowed for the application of decomposition and abstraction. Points and rewards were offered for the suitability of the proposed solutions, and a leaderboard was established allowing progress to be seen through the activities.

Sarah then structured the remaining lessons using a 'pathways' or 'storyline' approach that allowed her pupils to make decisions as to what 'route' they wanted to take in designing their game. Pupils could go into role and choose 'characters' to *play* the game. The 'character' choice determined the pathways they took in developing the game, the goals to achieve this, and creating their 'solution'. Logical reasoning, algorithmic understanding and automation all feature in this. So did pattern recognition with the commonly recurring aspects of games considered in both the game design and the pathway resources Sarah created for each 'character' to use. Again, underpinning this were various points-based rewards and motivational badges that were periodically added to the leaderboard to help secure the enthusiasm and engagement required. Prizes were awarded.

Sarah acknowledges that it took a lot of effort on her part to create the gamified experience that she wanted for her pupils. The different resources took time to produce and there was

→

additional time needed in using the points and reward techniques each lesson. However, she feels it was worth it and she now has the resources to reuse and adjust for other lessons. The pathways and characterisation approach allowed for effective differentiation. Her pupils really enjoyed this approach and the goals and challenge it set for them. The motivation and encouragement that the rewards and points added was excellent – although Sarah did have to remember to be inclusive in how she applied this. She also had to ensure that she did not get carried away with the excitement of the gamification pedagogy choices; the application of computational thinking also had to be made explicitly clear during the different phases of her pupils' learning.

Activity

Challenge yourself to develop a short scheme of work (see Chapter 10) that adopts either/both of:

- *Computational thinking by designing and coding a game.*
- *Computational thinking within gamification pedagogy.*

Ensure you embrace creative thinking and are very clear in how you are underpinning learning and progress by thinking computationally. Use the ideas presented in this chapter's case studies to help get you started.

Learning outcomes review

The aim of this chapter has been to get you thinking about using game design as a means of developing coding capability and computational thinking in your pupils, within the context of the Key Stage 1 and 2 computing curriculum. Positioning the pupils' programming and computational learning in the context of the familiar 'fun' and 'exciting' world of digital games would seem a sensible option in meeting the needs of the children in ways that will engage and support their progress. The purpose of the chapter has not been to tell you 'how' but to challenge you in using game design and gamification as tools to help deliver the computing curriculum – specifically aspects of computational thinking and coding.

Now you have engaged with this chapter's content, please review the learning outcomes from the perspective of your school-based placements and experiences so far:

- **Be familiar with the digital native/ digital immigrant debate and how this could inform your lesson planning in computing.**

(Continued)

(Continued)

> – In what ways is this influencing the way you and/ or your colleagues deliver their lessons – both in computing and other curriculum subjects? What challenges have you faced in trying to implement a more technologically familiar curriculum for your pupils?
>
> • **Consider how computational thinking is relevant in games design and how you could implement this in your teaching.**
>   – Having taught some coding lessons now, is placing programming learning in the context of game design the best way to establish the required learning? What benefits and pitfalls have you found in delivering lessons in this way?
>
> • **Identify with some current software platforms that can be used to deliver coding lessons through game creation.**
>   – What software have you used? Reflect on the learning and progress successes you achieved through the choices made.
>
> • **Review the use of gamification pedagogy and its links to thinking computationally.**
>   – Revisit the pedagogical thinking behind gamification and the theories underpinning it and summarise the main arguments and values being offered. If you have looked to adopt gamification methods in your classroom, identify the perceived impact it has had on motivation, performance and learning.

Further reading and resources

Kapp, K (2014) *'The Gamification of Learning and Instruction Fieldbook: Ideas into Practice'*. John Wiley and Sons.

A systematic guide to implementing the concepts and techniques of gamification from one of the world's leading experts in the field.

Livingstone, I and Hope, A (2011) *'Nesta: Next Gen Transforming the UK into the world's leading talent hub for the video games and visual effects industries'*. London: Nesta.

A seminal report that helped bring about computing curriculum change in its call for a transformation in the skills needed to develop video games in supporting the future of the UK's digital industries.

McGonigal, J (2011) *'Reality is Broken. Why Games Make Us Better and How They Can Change the World'*. London: Vintage Books.

Game designer, Jane McGonigal, considers games as transformational media and not just providing entertainment and play.

9 Computational Thinking Across the Curriculum

Learning outcomes

By the end of this chapter you should be able to:

- revise the key concepts and approaches involved in computational thinking;
- identify how computational thinking concepts and approaches can already be seen in daily classroom life;
- explore how the skills of computational thinking can enhance pupils' learning across a range of national curriculum subject areas;
- identify teaching, learning and assessment approaches which teachers can adopt to embed the promotion of computational thinking within lessons.

Teachers' Standards

A teacher must:

2. Promote good progress and outcomes by pupils:

- be aware of pupils' capabilities and their prior knowledge, and plan teaching to build on these;
- guide pupils to reflect on the progress they have made and their emerging needs;
- encourage pupils to take a responsible and conscientious attitude to their own work and study.

3. Demonstrate good subject and curriculum knowledge:

- have a secure knowledge of the relevant subject(s) and curriculum areas, foster and maintain pupils' interest in the subject, and address misunderstandings;
- demonstrate a critical understanding of developments in the subject and curriculum areas, and promote the value of scholarship.

4. Plan and teach well-structured lessons:

- promote a love of learning and children's intellectual curiosity;
- contribute to the design and provision of an engaging curriculum within the relevant subject area(s).

(DfE, 2011)

Introduction

As outlined earlier in Chapter 2, the development of children's computational thinking skills provides the foundation for the computing curriculum (DfE, 2013a). In addition to its clear links to computing, the potential of computational thinking to enhance learning across other curriculum areas also offers exciting opportunities. To recap, computational thinking encompasses a range of processes and approaches which can be utilised to tackle a problem or create a solution. Commonly used processes and approaches include:

Computational thinking processes:

- Logical reasoning – to predict, analyse and check information;
- Decomposition – breaking up problems into separate parts;
- Abstraction – removing irrelevant details;
- Pattern recognition or Generalisation – the identification and use of similarities;
- Algorithms – clear and precise step-by-step procedures or rules;
- Evaluation – ongoing decision making to check the solution meets the requirements of the problem.

Computational thinking approaches:

- Tinkering – experimenting and playing;
- Creating solutions;
- Debugging – finding and fixing errors;
- Perseverance;
- Collaboration.

(CAS Barefoot Computing, 2014)

It should be noted that computational thinking does not always require a computer and so-called 'unplugged' approaches should not be overlooked in developing children's approaches to problem solving (see Chapters 2 and 10 for more on unplugged approaches). This chapter will explore how and where computational thinking can already be seen in the classroom and how it can be applied to different subject areas. It should be noted that strong cross-curricular links between computing and other subjects have also been explored elsewhere in this book, for example, how floor robots can be used in geography and mathematics in Chapter 3. This chapter will also explore possible teaching, learning and assessment strategies which can be used to embed computational thinking across the curriculum.

Computational thinking in everyday classroom life

For teachers and pupils alike, computational thinking needs to be demystified and seen as a life skill used by everyone, not just computer scientists (Wing, 2006). While it may not be referred to using computing vocabulary, computational thinking processes are already present in many aspects of school life. In their daily lives, teachers will be providing algorithms, incorporating precise steps and rules for their pupils to follow. For example, when managing the transition at the end of an art lesson, the teacher will provide instructions on the tidying-up procedure, which pupils will follow by applying decomposition to break down the request into individual tasks, such as moving the artwork, clearing and cleaning the tables or tools. Abstraction skills will also be used to identify tasks to be prioritised over details which may not be relevant, for instance, all the paint bottles need to be put away, regardless of the colour. In addition, pupils will recognise patterns and similarities from previous routines and tasks which they can now apply or adjust when following the teacher's new request. There will no doubt be times when the tidying-up process may go wrong and need debugging by either the teacher or pupils, and of course, collaboration will be required.

Everyday examples of computational thinking processes in action may have no obvious relation to a computer or coding, but the use of such contexts helps teachers in understanding the technical terminology, as well as recognising that the skill set which computational thinking develops reaches far beyond the aims and requirements of the computing curriculum.

Activity: computational thinking in everyday school routines

During a typical school day, teachers or pupils may encounter or participate in the following events:

- Taking or responding to the morning attendance or lunch register;
- Lining up for assembly;
- Getting changed for physical education;
- Participating in a playground game;
- Selecting a meal in the school canteen;
- Fastening shoe laces;
- Dismissing pupils to parents, clubs or the school bus at the end of the day.

Identify which computational thinking processes and approaches may be used for the successful resolution or participation in each event. Go on to consider how each computational thinking process or approach is being used in each scenario.

Identify how the development of such skills links to the Key Stage 1 or 2 national curriculum for computing (DfE, 2013a). You may, of course, have your own routines or events which you wish to consider instead.

Planning for computational thinking across the curriculum

Historically, the use of ICT across a range of subject areas has been encouraged and was a national curriculum requirement in all subject areas (DfEE, 1999). In recent years there has been a shift away from ensuring pupils are prepared and trained to use technology to meet the demands of the future workplaces, towards developing a deeper understanding of the principles of computer science (DfE, 2013a).

On first glance, the subject content of the computing curriculum (DfE, 2013a) may appear discrete and difficult to deliver through a cross-curricular or embedded approach, however, once we begin to analyse and define the computing concepts under discussion, it can be seen that there is considerable scope for developing computational thinking in existing areas of other subjects, as well as identifying project-based cross-curricular approaches. Through identifying and promoting opportunities for computational thinking across different subject areas, pupils are provided with context and purpose for their learning and realise that the principles of computer science go way beyond learning to code towards using coding to learn how to think and solve problems (Resnick, 2013a).

When planning to apply computational thinking to other subject areas, teachers must carefully consider the purpose and learning outcomes of the lesson. It is important that the integrity and requirements of both subject areas are upheld. Where a cross-curricular approach is to be utilised, Desailly (2012) suggests that planning contains parallel learning objectives and pupils are clear on the learning outcomes for both subjects. Similarly, if the lesson primarily focuses on one subject, but there is opportunity to apply computational thinking skills within the teaching and learning approaches used, then teachers could signpost these links on their planning. Used regularly, approaches where planning and teaching show careful consideration of how computational thinking can be applied, will enable pupils to understand how such skills are transferable – and thus provide reciprocal benefits to both computing and other subjects. Planning for computational thinking is further explored in Chapter 10.

The following sections of this chapter will show where specific computational thinking processes and approaches can be seen in several different curriculum areas. It should be noted that this is not a fully comprehensive list of cross-curricular links, and readers are encouraged to identify further links which can be made in their own school's subject-based schemes of work (SoW).

Algorithms across the curriculum

Algorithms are precise step-by-step procedures and opportunities for pupils to develop their understanding of this area can be seen across a range of subject areas. In English, pupils will engage with instructional writing, story boarding, spelling rules and rhyming schemes in poetry – all of which require the application or creation of algorithms.

In mathematics, teachers will model algorithmic processes to pupils for tackling mathematical calculations and pupils will be familiar in using forms of algorithms such as RUCSAC to tackle word problems, where they will:

- **R**ead the problem
- **U**nderstand the requirements of the problem
- **C**hoose the correct mathematical operations and calculations
- **S**olve the calculations
- **A**nswer the original problem
- **C**heck the answer

In science, pupils' approach to scientific enquiry will require specific algorithmic processes to ensure fair testing principles are upheld. Furthermore, in identification and classification activities, children may follow or create databases, decision trees or flowcharts which require a procedural approach to be taken for identification, as can be seen in Figure 9.1.

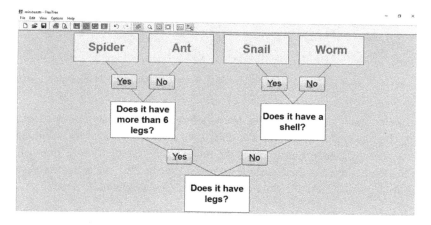

Figure 9.1 Decision tree algorithm created in FlexiTree 3

Physical Education also lends itself well to teaching and learning using an algorithmic-based approach. In dance and gymnastics, children will rehearse, refine and perform sequences showing that they have created or followed step-by-step procedures. In games, both in the playground and the sports field, children will begin to understand how rules and tactics impact on decision making within the algorithms present in competitive games.

Case study: using algorithms to create a relay obstacle course in P.E.

Primary PGCE trainee teachers visited Scargill Junior school in the London borough of Havering to observe how computing is embedded across different curriculum areas. During the visit the trainees were tasked with using a range of P.E. equipment to create a relay-based obstacle course for which a clear algorithm could be provided to human robots completing the course.

Figure 9.2 Planning an obstacle course

Working in small groups, the trainee teachers first planned and set up their obstacle course using the equipment which was available. They discussed how users would navigate the course and predicted any areas where the course may prove problematic or cause confusion to the user. Having refined the obstacle course and adopted the role of human robots to follow step-by-step instructions, the groups then recorded their algorithms on paper.

Recording of the algorithms on paper allowed the groups to further consider the clarity and precision of their instructions. As can be seen in Figure 9.3, a decision tree approach demonstrates where instructions were dependent on whether specific conditions had been met.

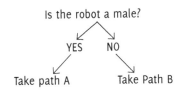

Figure 9.3 Recording an algorithm using a decision tree approach

The purpose and quality of such learning opportunities as outlined in this case study should be evaluated from both a computing and physical education perspective. It is clear that the activity linked to developing computational thinking, not just understanding of algorithms, but also logical reasoning, evaluation, decomposition, abstraction as well as encouraging collaborative working and debugging. Moreover, the algorithm itself could subsequently lead on to activities where pupils are programming floor robots to complete the course, or recreating the course using programming software.

Activity: planning for cross-curricular learning (P.E. and computing)

The value of the above activity in relation to computing is clearly apparent, however, we must also consider the activity's potential in relation to physical education (P.E.). From a P.E. perspective, this activity has the potential to encourage collaboration, competition, understanding of game rules and the opportunity for pupils to develop their movement and equipment skills, as well as ensuring pupils are *active for sustained periods of time* (DfE, 2013b).

Based on the activity described in the case study above, create a lesson plan (for any KS1 or KS2 year group) which contains parallel learning objectives for both computing and P.E. Further develop the lesson, so that having created the obstacle course, pupils are also developing their knowledge, skills and understanding in P.E.

Logical reasoning and evaluation across the curriculum

Logical reasoning and evaluation are key skills which pupils are expected to use across many subject areas, but in reality little time and attention is given to the development and teaching of these important concepts. Therefore, a cross-curricular approach to the teaching of computational thinking skills can support the teaching and learning of these valuable skills in a wide range of subject areas. In science, inference and prediction allow pupils to show their understanding of an investigation and allows teachers to assess the basis on which predictions have been made. For example, a child could be asked to predict whether the circuit below would work.

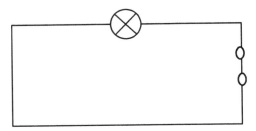

Figure 9.4 Incorrect circuit diagram

To ascertain whether the circuit is correct and will result in the bulb being lit, the child would be required to use a process of logical thinking, which may include processing the following questions:

- Is the circuit complete?
- Are all wires connected?
- Does the circuit have a bulb?
- Is the switch open or closed?
- Does the circuit contain a power source?

The child's ability to make a reasoned and accurate prediction would show understanding and application of prior knowledge to a new problem – a key logical thinking skill. In addition to developing logical reasoning through prediction opportunities in science, the conclusion to experiments offers substantial potential for teachers to facilitate discussion around findings, patterns, fair testing, variables and future investigations. A dialogic teaching approach would complement such discussions positively, and will be discussed later in this chapter.

Reasoning is a core skill of mathematics and allows pupils to show how they are using and applying their mathematical knowledge and understanding. The national curriculum for Mathematics, aims to ensure that all pupils:

> ...*reason mathematically by following a line of enquiry, conjecturing relationships and generalisations, and developing an argument, justification or proof using mathematical language.*

> (DfE, 2013c)

In addition, the curriculum recognises how mathematics is essential to other subject areas including technology, and clear similarities can be seen between reasoning, generalisation and proof in mathematics to the skills required in computational thinking.

Pattern recognition across the curriculum

Teachers will often ask pupils to identify and explain the patterns they can see – perhaps in number sequences, poems, music, graphs, results, artwork, spellings or words. Patterns are everywhere and lead to efficiency in problem solving as they assist in identifying common solutions and rules which can then be applied or adapted to other contexts in the form of a generalisation. As a teacher, you may have also identified patterns in pupil behaviour in specific contexts or environments, which can then be used to support in planning for positive learning behaviour in the future.

Younger pupils will begin their understanding of pattern recognition by identifying what is the same, and what is different through using concrete and picture-based experiences for simple sorting and classification activities. Children will then progress to other forms of pattern recognition such as those which can be seen in number classification (odd, even, prime, multiples, etc.) and sequences, or phonemes and spelling rules. In science, children will identify patterns in their results or interpretation of data to make predictions or reach conclusions. In music, pupils will develop their aural memory and composition skills through recognition of the repeating patterns within a piece and apply such structure to their own compositions. In art, children can analyse and identify patterns and motifs in famous artworks or architecture, and use block printing or software to create their own repeating patterns.

The ability to recognise, explain and work with patterns relies heavily on logical reasoning. Pattern recognition in mathematics may be visual or numeric. Either approach relies on the problem solver's logical reasoning to identify the pattern and relationships within the sequence, as well as the use of algorithms to continue or explain the pattern to others. Look at the growing shapes below:

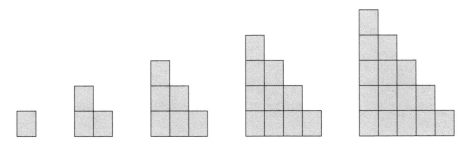

Figure 9.5 Pattern identification in growing shapes

- Can you draw the next shape in the sequence?
- How many squares will the next shape in the sequence contain?
- How many squares will the 10th shape in the sequence contain?
- How do you know?
- Can you explain the algorithm?
- What is the algorithm for the nth shape in the sequence?

Decomposition and abstraction across the curriculum

Decomposition and abstraction represent the ability to break a problem into smaller parts and recognising which details are relevant and those which can be ignored.

For example, when a teacher creates the weekly timetable for a class, both these processes are used to ensure the result is a concise, correctly structured timetable which is easy to read and follow. The labelling of diagrams is another example of where both decomposition and abstraction are used. When labelling diagrammatic representations, children are required to label only the key features and apply a process of decomposition to depict their understanding of different parts of the diagram.

In English, pupils will already be using decomposition in several ways, including their planning processes across different genres of writing. The use of writing or planning frames often supports in scaffolding the planning process for children as can be seen in Figure 9.6, which shows planning for a report or leaflet about a school (Palmer, 2001).

Whereas most planning for writing is often completed on paper, it should be noted that there are also real-time collaborative planning tools such as *Popplet* (**https://popplet.com/**), which uses a visual mind-mapping approach to support in breaking down the planning process and can be used individually or collaboratively.

In mathematics, word problems will often contain additional information which may not be essential to the required calculation or problem which needs to be solved. For example, in the

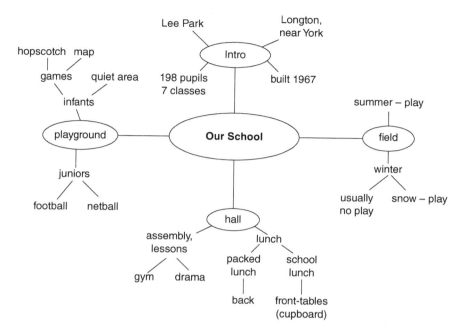

Figure 9.6 Report planning frame (Palmer, 2001)

following word problem, if pupils were to use the algorithmic approach RUCSAC, they would first read and understand the problem, during which an abstraction process would be required.

> Haleem is ten years old and he has £13.50 to share between 15 people for fizzy drinks in a café in London. What fraction of the money would each person receive? How much money would each person receive?

In this example, Haleem's age, the location of the café and choice of drinks may support understanding of the problem in providing context, but this information can be abstracted as unnecessary before going on to calculate, solve and answer the problem.

Activity: word problems and computational thinking

1) Create a set of word problems for either KS1 or KS2 pupils, where the following computational thinking skills can be encouraged:

- Decomposition – The problems will need to be broken down.
- Abstraction – There will be some unnecessary detail which needs to be removed from the problem.

(Continued)

(Continued)

- Algorithms – Pupils will follow the RUCSAC (read, understand, choose, solve, answer and check) acronym approach to tackling the problem.

2) Now, go on to consider your teaching input and modelling. How will you be able to model the use of these computational thinking processes? How will you adapt computational terminology to ensure language is age-appropriate and understood?

Computational thinking in design and technology

There are strong, long-standing links between the disciplines of computing, ICT and design and technology and although they are discrete subject areas they complement one another in many ways, for example, through computer-aided design and control technology. With increased focus on computational thinking, design and technology now offers further potential to make meaningful links between the two subject areas. The Royal Academy of Engineering (2014), recognises that design and technology offers practical contexts for children to advance their computational thinking and programming of physical systems in models and creations which they have planned, designed and invented. These types of palpable experiences allow pupils to truly understand the purpose and internal workings of their designs.

Design and technology is often taught in primary schools through a project-based approach, where children are set a design problem for which they must innovate a suitable solution. In the following case study, we can see how one teacher identified opportunities to embed computational thinking skills within a design and technology project.

Case study: computational thinking in design and technology

John is a Year 6 teacher and computing co-ordinator in a two form entry primary school. The school uses a creative curriculum approach where a topic-based approach is used for the teaching of foundation subjects. Last summer, the half-term topic for the year group was *'Friend or Foe'* based on Michael Morpurgo's (2011) children's book about a child's evacuation from London during the Second World War.

In design and technology, John planned for the class to look at shelters including those used during the war. Children were provided with the following brief for their design, make and evaluate project.

→

Design Brief: Working collaboratively in groups, you must design and make a small-scale shelter which is waterproof, windproof and able to withstand a weight of one kilogram being placed on its roof.

John planned a 'shelters'-themed SoW to be carried out over the period of a six-week half-term. While planning the sequence of lessons, he identified where computational thinking skills could be developed through the design, make and evaluate process. The following week-by-week breakdown shows how each week's design and technology focus was complemented with an additional computational thinking (CT) focus:

Table 9.1 Design and Technology topic overview showing links to computational thinking.

Week	Design and Technology focus	Computation thinking links
1	Children to sort pictures to identify different types of shelters and their purpose.	• Logical Reasoning: Discussion and questioning to recognise the key features and requirements of shelters. • Abstraction: Some pictures will contain additional details which are not core requirements for shelters – which details can be ignored?
2	Research and evaluate the suitability of different materials for shelters.	• Tinkering: Allowing children to experiment and explore the range of materials. • Logical Reasoning and Evaluation: Discussion and explanation regarding the suitability of specific materials over others.
3	Collaboratively plan and design a shelter which meets specific requirements.	• Decomposition: Breaking the problem into stages from planning through to completion of the project. • Collaboration: Which roles and rules are required for the group? How will decisions and disagreements be managed? • Creating: Children have the opportunity to innovate and design creative solutions to the given problem.
4	Share design diagrams and collaborative evaluation.	• Collaboration: Groups share their designs with others and feedback is used to evaluate and adapt the ongoing design process. • Debugging and Perseverance: Feedback on design may present new challenges for groups which will require adaptations to be made or potential flaws to be corrected.
5	Select appropriate materials and tools to construct shelters.	• Algorithms: In following a design, children will need to establish an order of events for creating the shelter. Precise instructions may also be required in the use of specific tools.
6	Testing and evaluation of shelters against the original brief criteria.	• Pattern Recognition: During testing, children will recognise patterns and make generalisations regarding which shelters or materials were most successful and why. • Evaluation: Groups will evaluate their shelters against the original requirements of the brief and identify how their design can be improved.

→

To ensure the computational thinking connections were explicit to pupils, John also carefully considered the teaching and learning strategies he used. In addition to modelling of computational thinking processes, collaborative, dialogic and inquiry-based learning approaches were amongst the strategies used to develop pupils' problem solving skills during the project.

Activity: identifying cross-curricular opportunities for computational thinking.

Year 2 children are learning about The Great Fire of London as their cross-curricular topic for the half term. Create a topic web which shows cross-curricular links for how this topic could link to learning opportunities in the following subject areas:

- History
- Computing
- Geography
- Science
- Design & Technology

You are free to consider other subject areas if you wish to do so. Now go on to show how computational thinking processes and approaches can be embedded throughout the learning opportunities across the full range of different subject areas (not just computing).

Debugging across the curriculum and Assessment for Learning (AfL)

Along with tinkering, creating, persevering and collaborating – debugging is seen as a computational thinking approach rather than a process. Debugging requires programmers to spot and correct errors within their programming. Debugging in the classroom and across the curriculum may be known under many other names, but the fundamental method of checking and correcting work is commonplace across many subject areas. Self-assessment and peer-assessment is often seen in lessons, where children will review their work against the learning outcomes or success criteria, as well as identifying strengths and areas for development. In English, this may include the proofreading of written work and in mathematics the checking of calculations.

Debugging is an essential skill in computing and programming but can be both time consuming and a challenge to one's perseverance. Drawing on Seymour Papert's work, Carver and Klahr (1986) argue that children are often reluctant to debug and prefer to start over because they simply do not know how to, as the skill of debugging is not taught. Debugging, in a different form, can already be seen in other commonplace classroom activities such as the proofreading and the checking of calculations. Such approaches are often identified as assessment for learning strategies, where pupils take a leading role and teachers are expected to guide pupils to reflect on their progress and encourage a conscientious attitude towards study (DfE, 2011).

AfL encompasses a range of assessment strategies which aim to involve pupils actively in the learning journey through effective dialogue and feedback which is used to close the achievement gap between prior and new learning. Dylan Wiliam (2006) outlines the five core strategies of assessment for learning as:

- understanding of the learning intentions and success criteria;
- engineering effective classroom discussions, questions and tasks that elicit evidence of learning;
- providing feedback that moves learners forward;
- activating students as instructional resources for each other, and
- activating students as owners of their own learning.

Self and peer-assessment provide a valuable opportunity for pupils to learn from one another, as well as checking and understanding of success criteria. This form of assessment or evaluation is already used in the classroom in the form of checking work against success criteria and providing constructive feedback across a range of subject areas. The expected skills which pupils use to underpin their assessment and evaluation of learning is in many ways a process of debugging, where content is checked, errors (or improvements) are identified and then acted upon. Within computational thinking, the use of logical reasoning and evaluation in debugging also requires an understanding of what is expected, so that errors can be identified, understood and corrected. While this could be achieved by providing individual pupils with a procedural approach or checklist for the debugging process, a peer-assessment approach would also be beneficial and offer additional insight. Whichever approach is used, a positive classroom climate is key to enable pupils to understand that making and debugging errors is part of the learning process.

Research focus: dialogic teaching and computational thinking

The intangible nature of computational thinking processes and approaches makes it a difficult concept for some to define or meaningfully apply to a range of subjects, and for some it is viewed as a discrete set of skills (The British Computing Society, 2007). While this chapter presents ideas for how and where computational thinking can be seen in a range of different subject areas, putting these ideas into practice draws upon a teacher's wider repertoire

→

of teaching strategies to ensure that children's engagement with computational thinking is facilitated and evident. One such strategy worthy of consideration here is that of dialogic teaching.

Dialogic teaching (Alexander, 2008), utilises talk for learning and moves away from so-called 'teacher talk' towards interactive discussion between teachers and pupils. Dialogic teaching uses talk in specific forms to further pupils' understanding and learning in topics, and enables the teacher to assess progress and comprehension. Dialogic teaching in science has also shown that pupil engagement and motivation increased when their ideas and views were incorporated and appreciated through discussion (Mercer *et al.*, 2009). Alexander's (2008) framework differentiates between dialogic teaching and everyday question and answer exchanges in the classroom environment, through requirements which include:

- questions that are used to stimulate thinking and should be cognitively challenging;

- answers which require reasoning and should be further developed through discussion;

- teacher feedback should lead to further development of thinking and not just stop at praise or acceptance;

- discussion should develop coherently along specific lines of enquiry;

- the classroom environment should provide a safe and welcoming climate for such discussions to take place.

Dialogic teaching provides an ideal approach to embedding computational thinking across the curriculum as many computational processes require discussion and questioning to ascertain how they are being used and understood. For example, while it may be evident through written work that a child has decomposed a mathematical problem and used an algorithm to complete a written calculation, the truer representation of the child's understanding of the processes involved can be gained through discussion. Similarly, a child could write down their predictions or describe identified patterns in a science lesson, but a dialogic approach would provide greater insight.

Activity: using dialogic teaching to promote computational thinking

Reflect back to a lesson (in any subject area) where teaching and learning may have touched upon opportunities for pupils to develop their computational thinking skills. If you were to deliver this lesson again, which dialogic teaching strategies could you use to stimulate discussion to facilitate and assess children's computational thinking?

Learning outcomes review

This chapter has explored how computational thinking can be seen and developed in a range of different subject areas and contexts. Some subject areas such as science, mathematics and design and technology offer clear links and opportunities for pupils to transfer their skills and knowledge to a range of different contexts. This chapter has also acknowledged that computational thinking processes may not always be apparent as concrete or recordable events, therefore, teaching and assessment strategies must incorporate dialogic and evaluative approaches which provide opportunities for pupils to show their understanding. Thinking about a school with which you are familiar, reflect on the questions below in relation to each learning outcome from this chapter.

- **Revise the key concepts and approaches involved in computational thinking.**
  Revisit your understanding of computational thinking processes and approaches by writing your own definition for each term. Consider how you would explain these terms to children in both KS1 and 2.

- **Identify how computational thinking concepts and approaches can already be seen in daily classroom life.**
  Reflect on a recent school day, how did you or your pupils use computational thinking processes and approaches?

- **Explore how the skills of computational thinking can enhance pupils' learning across a range of national curriculum subject areas.**
  Looking back on the lessons which you delivered this week (or most recent school week), identify opportunities where computational thinking processes and approaches could have been promoted in the lessons.

- **Identify teaching, learning and assessment approaches which teachers can adopt to embed the promotion of computational thinking within lessons.**
  Reflect on your use of questioning – which types of questions could be used to develop pupils' logical reasoning, evaluation skills and perseverance with debugging activities.

Further reading and resources

(Additional resources are listed in Chapter 2)

BBC Bitesize – Computational Thinking

Available at: **www.bbc.co.uk/education/topics/z7tp34j** (accessed 17 February 2017).

Although these resources are intended for Key Stage 3, they provide ideal subject knowledge resources for primary teachers. The website includes learner guides and video clips which can be used in the classroom.

Computing at School (CAS)

Computational Thinking – A Guide for Teachers (2015). Available at:

https://community.computingatschool.org.uk/files/6695/original.pdf (accessed 17 February 2017).

This guide provides a conceptual framework for understanding computational thinking in the computing curriculum, as well as providing practical guidance on how it can be delivered in the classroom.

10 Planning for Computational Thinking and Coding

Learning outcomes

By the end of this chapter you will have:

- considered the importance of planning for computational thinking and coding;
- considered teaching the progression of computational thinking and coding skills;
- become familiar with how to identify opportunities for planning computational thinking and coding as a subject in its own right and within other curriculum areas.

Teachers' Standards

A teacher must:

1. Set high expectations which inspire, motivate and challenge pupils:

- set goals that stretch and challenge pupils of all backgrounds, abilities and dispositions.

2. Promote good progress and outcomes by pupils:

- plan teaching to build on pupils' capabilities and prior knowledge.

3. Demonstrate good subject and curriculum knowledge:

- have a secure knowledge of the relevant subject(s) and curriculum areas, foster and maintain pupils' interest in the subject, and address misunderstandings.

4. Plan and teach well-structured lessons:

- promote a love of learning and children's intellectual curiosity;
- reflect systematically on the effectiveness of lessons and approaches to teaching;
- contribute to the design and provision of an engaging curriculum within the relevant subject area(s).

5. Adapt teaching to respond to the strengths and needs of all pupils:

- know how to adapt teaching to support pupils' education at different stages of development;
- have a clear understanding of the needs of all pupils.

6. Make accurate and productive use of assessment:

- use relevant data to monitor progress, set targets, and plan subsequent lessons.

(DfE, 2011)

Introduction

Although this chapter is concerned with planning for computational thinking and coding, many of the principles of good planning in general still apply and will not be covered here. During your placements you will most likely be expected to plan using a format given to you. These proformas provide you with the headings and prompts of the elements you need to plan for and it is unlikely you will be allowed to teach a class of children without one.

Before we begin it is worth considering not just the reasons behind planning, but what makes a plan a good plan.

Activity: why plan?

Write down all the reasons why teachers need to plan. From your list try putting the items into order of importance.

Using your list(s) from above as a starting point, write down six key things which are characteristic of successful learning objectives. When you have done this, compare your lists with those on page 151 of this chapter. Consider these points both in terms of teaching computational thinking and coding and how they would apply in each primary age phase.

Research focus: planning for twenty-first century learners

It is important not just to think about what you will plan and teach but rather a consideration of *who* you will be teaching and planning for. The need to equip pupils for life in the twenty-first century has become something of a platitude in the media, in industry, global politics and in education but what this actually means or entails is hard to pin down. The terms global citizen, digital foot print, sustainability and digital literacy may crop up with frequency and although what pupils should actually learn remains nebulous, it is clear that we should be teaching children *for* and not *about* the twenty-first century (Hicks, 2006; Hicks and Holden, 1995).

Within this context, Patterson (2016) draws upon the descriptors from The Framework for 21st Century Learning (P21, 2016) and aligns the skills of the twentieth-century learner with those pupils need for today. He considers that the disciplines of compliance and timeliness translate themselves into learning and innovation skills. He sees basic literacy as a natural migration into information, media and technology skills and perceives the notion of community involvement extending to encompass life and career skills.

Many of the attributes in the P21 (Partnership for 21st Century Learning) Framework should resonate with you as a good number of them intersect closely with the characteristics associated with computing and computational thinking. These twenty-first century skills can be mapped onto the computing curriculum which comprises three main strands – computer science [CS], Information Technology [IT] and Digital Literacy [DL]. The table below takes the skills for the twenty-first century (P21, 2016) and aligns them with strands and themes from the computing national curriculum (Berry, 2015; DfE, 2013a):

Table 10.1 Mapping twenty-first century skills with the computing national curriculum

Twenty-first century skills	Computing and computational thinking skills
Learning and innovation skills	
Creativity and innovation	Create digital content (IT)
	Create and debug programs (CS)
Critical thinking and problem solving	Use logical reasoning to explain how algorithms work (CS)
	Use sequence, selection & repetition in programs (CS)
Communication and collaboration	Work together to detect and correct errors in algorithms (CS)
	Work together in creating digital content (IT)
Information, media and technology skills	
Information literacy	Use decomposition, abstraction & debugging when coding (CS)
	Appreciate how search results are selected and ranked (CS)
Media literacy	Understand the multiple services of the internet (CS)
ICT literacy	Organise, store, manipulate and retrieve digital content (IT)
Life and career skills	
Flexibility and adaptability	Recognise common uses of information technology beyond school (DL)
Initiative and self-direction	Evaluate digital content (DL)
	Use search technologies effectively (IT)
Leadership and responsibility	Use technology safely, respectfully and responsibly (DL)

Although computational thinking skills and coding will be disciplines that pupils will need to learn, perhaps the most important thing is to consider the world of uncertainty pupils will be growing up in. To deal with change pupils will need to know how to be flexible and although collaborative skills will be important, as a teacher you will need to plan for them to learn self-directional skills for a workplace where they may be unmanaged yet accountable for their productivity and output (Patterson, 2016).

An overview of planning

Long-term planning

Long-term planning often equates with a specific subject scheme of work [SoW], in this case, computing. The principal job of a SoW is to break down the progression of learning across year groups and age phases usually by term and by year to show broadly what will be taught and what pupils will learn. Characteristically, it lacks the detail of lesson plans and will often contain only brief descriptions of each unit of work.

Computing schemes are usually governed by the computing strands – CS, IT and DL. However, the way content is mapped or grouped may vary between schools. Planning and teaching may therefore be conceived and structured in different ways, as in the example below:

Table 10.2 Strands within computing schemes of work

Computing scheme themes – School A	Computing scheme themes – School B
Algorithms	Deciphering and interpreting with technology
Programming and development	Inquiring and communicating with technology
Data and data representation	Creating and composing with technology
Hardware and processing	Operating and mastering technology
Information Technology	

To illustrate how the themes above might align, a Year 2 unit of work using Scratch, for example, would fit with *'programming and development'* in school A and *'deciphering and interpreting with technology'* in school B. Examples of different SoWs can be found on the CAS community website (see the activity below).

Another factor which may determine how a SoW is conceived, constructed and implemented is the extent to which computing is embedded across the curriculum, or taught as a discrete subject in its own right. With the previous ICT national curriculum (DfE, 1999) there was a strong case for adopting a cross-curricular approach in which technology could be integrated in a meaningful way. With the new curriculum this is perceived to be more challenging because of the greater level of discrete subject knowledge, but this should not preclude the many opportunities to apply computational thinking to other subject areas (Berry, 2015). Either way, the planning and teaching of computational thinking and coding should invariably lend itself towards the progression of learning.

Rising Stars' (2016) 'Switched on Computing' scheme provides a useful map of what a computing scheme overview looks like. You can see clearly how the units of work map out and develop from Year 1 to Year 6 – **www.risingstars-uk.com/media/Rising-Stars/ soc2ndeditiongrid_newJuly16.pdf**. Additionally, the Computing at School [CAS] Community (see activity below) offers a wide range of resources to support the planning and teaching of computing.

Activity: evaluating Schemes of Work

Using the computing SoW from your school as a starting point, carry out the following activity:

1. Sign up to the CAS Community **http://community.computingatschool.org. uk/**
2. Search for 'computing schemes of work'. Some schemes will be year group or key stage specific, others may span across key stages. The 'Primary Curriculum Scheme' created by Dale Coan and Paul Browning (**http://community. computingatschool.org.uk/resources/4533**) provides a good, coherent example adapted from Rising Stars 'Switched on Computing' although there are many other examples.
3. Browse and download a few examples. Then, for a year group of your choice, compare your own scheme to consider how they have:

   a) Identified the three strands: *computer science* [CS], *information technology* [IT] and *digital literacy* [DL] and map these against content/learning activities.
   b) Demonstrated progression of concepts and skills through tasks and activities within units and across the year group.
   c) Used resources such as hardware, software, online content and unplugged resources to support learning.
   d) Approached and identified assessment for learning e.g. through Progression Pathways "I can…" statements and CAS digital badges.

In addition, you may want to extend the above activity across year groups and Key Stages.

Medium-term planning

Medium-term planning will usually consist of a unit or block of work drawn from the school's SoW. As a beginning teacher, it will often be the medium-term plans that you will be given in order to plan in detail the sequence of lessons over the course of your placement. Medium-term plans should demonstrate development and progression in concepts and/or skills, knowledge and/or experiences. See Table 10.3 (below) for an example of a medium-term plan for a unit of work on Logo:

Table 10.3 An example of medium-term planning

Year 4 – Programming with Logo						
Week 1	Week 2	Week 3	Week 4	Week 5	Week 6	Week 7
Introduce Logo. Remind them of Scratch and difference in block code and script. Show them the basic commands to create simple designs.	Give children a series of commands and get them to predict what the code will do then test out their hypotheses. Give them errant code for shapes for them to debug.	Introduce the repeat command and use of brackets []. Show them how to create shapes using repeat and applying the Turtle Theorem (Turn × Angle = 360)	Show them how to build a one-word procedure for a shape and how to use editor to do this. Remind them how Logo doesn't save primitives. Get them to save Logo file and their procedures.	Show the children how to write a program to create a shape pattern using a procedure within a procedure i.e. the program for the shape as part of the procedure for the pattern.	Introduce setpc command and code for Logo colours. Ask them to create a program for a shape pattern containing procedures for three coloured shapes.	Assessment week.

The finer points of planning concerning lesson structure, grouping, differentiation, meeting individual needs, finer details of the activities and assessment of them or the role of other adults are not included in medium-term plans. How you go about executing each segment of learning is down to you and the dynamics and nature of the children in your class will determine many of the finer points on your short-term plans.

Short-term planning

Short-term planning is often synonymous with individual lesson plans and unlike the other types of planning it requires higher levels of attention to detail and can therefore be a time consuming process. The internet provides a wealth of 'ready to use' lesson plans and teaching materials and it is very easy to simply print off and use these resources. However great the temptation, you should first ask yourself a number of questions. To begin with, where does the material comes from? Does it come from another country and education system or context different to your own? If you are going to use it, then how will you adapt it to suit the different needs of your children and what you need to teach? Where does the activity sit within the wider picture of your school's computing scheme? Will it form part of a sequence of lessons or is it only useful for a stand-alone lesson? If the resource you have chosen will involve copying 30 identical worksheets, then are you adequately meeting the needs of every learner?

Lesson planning

Earlier in this chapter, you will have formulated ideas about what makes a lesson plan a good plan. Many of the features you will have identified should arise naturally through ensuring you have addressed all components of your lesson planning pro-forma. In Table 10.4 (below) these aspects are considered in the context of planning which involves computational thinking and/or coding. As you read through you may wish to consider how they would apply to one of the Year 4 lesson outlines above (Table 10.3).

Table 10.4 Considerations for planning to teach computing

Aspect of lesson plan	Considerations for teaching computing
Subject, year group, date, no. of children	The number of children may well inform pairings or groupings if using computers or other devices. If it is a year group new to you, what experiences of computational thinking and coding have they had previously?
Learning objectives/ success criteria	Are these specific and measurable and suitably challenging for all pupils? Are they matched to Computing Progression Pathways assessment statements or other similar ways of measuring learning outcomes? If the lesson forms part of other subject teaching, have you ensured that the learning objectives are suitably matched to computing? Are you clear about the difference between objectives (what you would *like* them to learn) and outcomes (what they *actually* learned? (Grigg, 2010, p.245).
Previous learning	This may not just be to do with the last lesson on Bee-Bots or using Scratch. It might also be related to pupils' skills of estimation or reasoning developed in maths and therefore computational skills, and if so, which ones? It may also relate to whether there are any misconceptions that need to be addressed or pupils who need extending.
National curriculum references	These should be drawn from the computing PoS and should marry up with the learning outcomes and reflect the content of the lesson. They can also include reference to NC aims for example if pupils are applying what they know in one technology to understand another. Even if you are in the EYFS some KS1 objectives may still apply.
Assessment/ pupil progress	Assessment in computing is more often likely to be based on observations of what children are doing rather than monitoring what they have written in their books. If children are sharing technologies how will you know what each child can do individually? If you have another adult with you, what role will they play in assessment? Of fundamental importance is the question: *What evidence do I have that shows that all pupils have made good progress?*
Resources	Has functionality of equipment been checked? Will equipment need charging beforehand? If you are planning on using the internet or network do you have a contingency plan (pencil and paper alternative) in case it is not working?

(Continued)

145

Table 10.4 (Continued)

Aspect of lesson plan	Considerations for teaching computing
Key vocabulary	This may include technical words or terms which you need to ensure you know and use correctly. For example, it is important that children know that HTML is not a programming language and that the internet is not the same as the world wide web. It may also include acronyms that will need to be spelled out.
Differentiation/ personalising learning/pupil progress	Technology generally lends itself well in assisting how learning can be adjusted to meet the balance between personalisation and differentiation of learning (Bray and McClaskey, 2013). For example, using Roamer Too allows pupils to engage with different interfaces of varying complexity. Similarly, consideration will need to be given to how, and at what levels, pupils engage with writing their own programs or use computer software.
	It is important to remember that programming skills can be acquired visually and that programs can be written/recorded using symbols and numbers and that programming itself is a tactile process. In these ways it can be easily accessed for those pupils who have EAL or Special Educational Needs [SEN]. Conversely, extending higher attaining pupils can readily be achieved by accessing and using higher levels of coding e.g. using CSS in HTML. Similarly, if pupils are conversant with one particular platform e.g. Scratch, they can be set the challenge of producing the same algorithm in another language (Berry, 2015).
Lesson structure	Lesson length and structure may vary depending on the school you are in and may not always follow the tripartite format. For example, lessons may begin with a practical investigation or exploration and there may be mid-lesson plenaries for points of review rather than at the end. If you do plan a tripartite lesson, ensure that introductions are not overlong and that enough time is given over to practical activity. You will also need to plan in time to set up, hand out and collect in equipment. Being logged into a network and/or having programs already open and ready to use can save time.
Role of other adults	Making sure other adults are briefed about their role in the lesson is vital. Where possible they should be familiar with any programs you are using or any computational concepts, key vocab or resources you are introducing to the children. They can also play a key role is assessing pupils and you will need to plan for and manage this.
Lesson evaluation	Reflecting upon and evaluating your teaching is an important part of the planning cycle and this process involves moving through the following stages:
	Plan → Teach → Assess → Review
	Evaluating a lesson has far more to it than 'What went well?' and 'What I could improve?' In reflecting upon your teaching, your overarching aim should be focused on improving outcomes for pupils and perhaps one of the most fundamental questions you will need to ask yourself – and your pupils – before and after each lesson is why is computational thinking so important? (Berry, 2013b, p.4).

Case study: planning in the EYFS

Jadine is a trainee in an EYFS setting. She is aware of the computing curriculum but has told her university tutor that *they don't teach it [computing]. It's not statutory here [EYFS]. There is some ICT and we use the computer suite but it's not a priority in the nursery although I am*

→

trying to use it to support learning. I think the older kids in the school might do programming and computational thinking but we don't do it with the younger ones down here.

This is a plan Jadine shared with her tutor:

Table 10.5 EYFS lesson plan

EYFS Lesson Plan: Adult-directed activity			
Name of trainee: Jadine	Date/Time: 28/6/16 (am)	Area of learning/EYFS framework: Mathematics/Understanding the World	Year group: Nursery
Learning outcome/s: • To click and drag the fruit into the boxes • To write their name onscreen using the keyboard **Previous learning** As part of their topic on food children have had experience of shopping for food, cooking and eating. They have been listening to stories and rhymes about food. The children in the nursery have fruit snack times each day. Nursery children are timetabled for a weekly half hour session in the ICT suite. They attend in groups of 10-12		Key vocabulary • Keyboard • Mouse • Screen • Click • Drag • Sort	Resources • A selection of fruit: Bananas, pears, oranges, apples, plums (a few of each) • 4–5 trays • Laminated labels with children's names • Computers • Interactive whiteboard • MyWorld software (sorting fruit screen)

Description of activity:

Previous preparation

Teacher to log children on to the network, load MyWorld on each screen and place a laminated name card on the keyboards. Teacher loads software on teaching computer. Place the selection of fruit randomly on the carpet. Have the trays ready by the door.

- Arrive with the children.
- Open the door and step back with amazement. "Oh, look! Some silly person has dropped all this fruit and left it on the floor!"
- Ask children if they can help me pick up the fruit and put the fruit in the trays.
- Talk as you go "there's another banana over there."
- Hold up the fruit and ask the children if they know what each one is called, who has tried one?
- Sitting at the teaching computer hold up the mouse then keyboard, point to the computer screen.
- Ask children if they know the name for each piece of equipment.
- Ask children to repeat the names after you.

Show pupils the MyWorld Sorting screen.

- Make some connections to earlier on pointing out the trays and the fruit on screen.
- Ask children if they know what I'm going to do.
- Model how to click and drag items of fruit into the trays. Model the language. "I'm going to **click** on this pear and **drag** it over to this tray."
- Discuss how it might be a good idea to put the bananas together. How many oranges are in this tray?

Hold up a laminated pupil's name card and fix it to the keyboard with Blu-tak so they can see.

- Model how to write their name on screen.
- Hold the keyboard so they can see and carefully type the letters of your name.
- Ask children if they would like to have a go.
- Show children to their places pointing out their name card.

Ask Kim (TA) or Ali (helper) to supervise half the group while you work with the other half.

- JA and CP might struggle with their mouse control. Ask TA to support by guiding their hand on occasion.

Most children will work independently and will click and drag the fruit randomly into the trays. Some will complete the screen and will have sorted the fruit by type.

- Remind pupils to have a go at writing their name.
- Monitor PK and LO to see if they write their names.
- FG, ML, GH might complete the task – give them blocks screen as extension.
- Ask the children to come back on the carpet. Tell them Kim will save their work for them.
- Repeat the show and name activity from the introduction to the lesson.
- BD (EAL) might need to model activity for her first.
- Hold up the keyboard and ask pupils if they can see a letter in their name.
- Ask one or two to come up and show you.

Show them the fruit they picked up earlier. Explain that when the fruit has been washed and cut up they'll be able to have some later on when they have their fruit snack.

Points to note

It is not important if they don't complete the screen or write their name. They should be encouraged to engage with the activity but not coerced.

Some pupils may close the sorting screen and choose another. This should be discussed positively with the child.

Some pupils may have very limited or no mouse skills at all.

MyWorld Screen

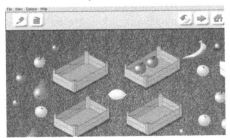

Figure 10.1 The sorting screen

Activity: lesson evaluation

Read through Jadine's plan and then respond to the prompts and questions below:

1. Referring to the computing curriculum (DfE, 2013a) and Chapter 2 of this book, what opportunities are there to introduce concepts and experiences of computational thinking? Have any previous opportunities been missed?
2. To what extent has the plan taken into account all the considerations for teaching computing lessons outlined in Table 10.4? Are there any aspects of planning missing or any extraneous information?
3. How might the curriculum references be altered or changed to better reflect the statutory framework for the EYFS (DfE, 2014) as well as the Development Matters EYFS framework (BAECE, 2012) and possibly the computing curriculum (DfE, 2013a)? Consider what detail could be added to this section of the plan.
4. Could the key vocabulary be tinkered with to include words or terms to reflect the development of computational thinking skills that this lesson activity could provide?
5. How could the learning objectives be improved? As they stand, they are more focused on what the children will do rather than what they will learn. Are there any learning outcomes not identified which could be linked explicitly to computational thinking objectives?

Planning to teach computational thinking and coding in the EYFS

Some local authority Grids for Learning (GfLs) such as Hertfordshire provide a computing scheme to include the EYFS which identifies enabling environments where pupils develop skills with using input devices and engage in phonics and number games with a view to developing their skills of matching and ordering and describing patterns (Herts for Learning, 2016). Clare Nevinson provides a model of an Early Years computing SoW which is useful because it maps skills and activities against the three computing strands (CS, IT and DL) and includes the files and resources needed: (**http://community.computingatschool.org.uk/ resources/3726**).

ScratchJr (see Chapter 4) is predominantly aimed at pupils in KS1 but there are some (e.g. Alina Manda, **http://community.computingatschool.org.uk/resources/3071**) who advocate children in the EYFS use iPads and ScratchJr to develop the concepts of programming, instructions, sequencing as well as introducing blocks into the scripting area.

Planning for computational thinking and coding in the EYFS requires you to look at the statutory framework (DfE, 2014) to identify where opportunities may arise other than within children's experience of technology. For example, how the six concepts of computational thinking identified by CAS Barefoot Computing (2014) align with early learning goals:

- Listening to stories and anticipating events (**Logic**)
- Recognising, creating and describing patterns (**Algorithms**)
- Engagement in de-coding in phonics and instructions in communication and language (**Decomposition**)
- Doubling and halving numbers in maths (**Patterns**)
- Identifying similarities and differences between objects, places and materials in understanding the world (**Abstraction and Evaluation**).

As with the lesson evaluation activity (p.149) you will need to identify how you are going to introduce these concepts, approaches, skills and the associated vocabulary with the children.

Although non-statutory, the 'Development Matters' (British Association for Early Childhood Education (BAECE), 2012) guidance provides some excellent and extremely useful material in exemplifying how teaching might look like in the different areas of learning. A simple example, or illustration, of identifying patterns might be modelling threading different coloured beads onto a piece of string, discussing them with children and letting them make their own:

Figure 10.2 Exploring patterns with beads

A simple search of the 'Development Matters' guidance for the word 'patterns' comes up with twenty results with some interesting and creative examples/ideas. Try it:

www.foundationyears.org.uk/files/2012/03/Development-Matters-FINAL-PRINT-AMENDED.pdf

Planning to teach computational thinking and coding unplugged (5–11)

KS1

It is important to remember that the availability of the computer suite or tablets does not necessarily restrict the teaching of computing and that it is possible to plan a number of CT/

coding objectives in an 'unplugged' way. The CAS Barefoot website (**http://barefootcas.org.uk/**) provides a useful starting point although the site requires you to register first. It is a good idea to be clear about what aspect(s) of computing you are planning to teach before entering the website and searching for resources, and remember they will need to be tailored to the pupils' needs in your class. The links to the computational thinking concepts are helpful in this respect and offer guidance, explanations and examples of how each one may look like in the primary curriculum.

The CAS Quickstart Computing toolkit (**www.quickstartcomputing.org/**) is broken down into sections which can be misleading as the section on 'planning guidance' is not the best place to look for potential activities or resources. It is perhaps better for you to select other sections, for example 'computational thinking' or 'programming'.

Although they do not offer the same level of detail or structure provided by Barefoot, the Quickstart guide contains a range of plugged as well as unplugged ideas and starting points.

Finally, it is worth considering any unplugged games which may be available in your classroom cupboard. For example, Scrabble, Connect 4 or the code-breaking game Mastermind all offer tactile and visual experiences which support the teaching of the concepts of logic, algorithms, and patterns.

KS2

Much of the above concerning Barefoot and the CAS Quickstart materials applies to Key Stage 2. When planning to teach 'unplugged', it is worth also considering pencil and paper versions of games such as Minesweeper or teaching pupils Morse Code, British Sign Language or how to play chess. Non-verbal reasoning tests also practise skills related to computational thinking.

You are encouraged not to see the curriculum as a limit to what you can plan to teach but as an opportunity to be adventurous and there are some schemes of work which include, for example, units on cryptography (Berry, 2015). Lewis Carroll's Red Shift code is a good example of this and is featured in children's author, Alan Garner's books **http://alangarner. atspace.org/table.html**.

Although caution will be needed in selecting and presenting appropriate clips for pupils to watch, an inspiring way to introduce work on coding or encryption might be to show part of a movie trailer for example, *The Imitation Game* **https://www.youtube.com/ watch?v=nuPZUUED5uk**.

Planning lists from the lesson plan activity on p.140

Why do we plan?

- demonstrate curriculum coverage and subject knowledge;
- demonstrate progression in learning;

- promote high expectations of our pupils;
- meet the needs of every learner in the best way possible;
- provide a balance of challenge and support;
- manage time effectively;
- facilitate appropriate choice of resources and approaches;
- personalise learning in response to the child;
- build upon previous learning experiences;
- show how assessment informs what is taught;
- ensure children are clear about what they are learning (and why);
- demonstrate a match between what has been planned and what actually takes place.

Characteristics of successful learning objectives:

- short and focused;
- suitably challenging for all pupils;
- consistent with the 'bigger picture';
- shared at the start and provide a point of reference during lessons;
- build upon previous learning;
- provide purpose to the lesson;
- presented in a language easy for children to understand;
- focused on learning, e.g. WALT (We Are Learning To ...)
- provide success criteria and guide assessment for learning;
- are SMART (Specific, Measurable, Attainable, Realistic, Time-bound);
- matches activities to learning outcomes.

Learning outcomes review

This chapter considered aspects and features of different planning formats and the requirements and purposes for different levels of planning. You will have reflected upon a range of content and resources that could be used to teach pupils computing across the primary age range.

Thinking about a school you know, consider the following questions in reviewing your knowledge and understanding of the content in this chapter:

(Continued)

(Continued)

- **Considered the pedagogical importance of planning and the implications this has for teaching children computational thinking and coding across the primary age range.**
  Reflect on the extent to which your planning has addressed the considerations for teaching computing outlined in Table 10.4. What evidence is there to indicate that pupils are self-directed and independent in their learning of concepts and approaches to computing and computational thinking?

- **Become familiar with the different forms that planning takes and the implications this has for teaching the progression of computational thinking and coding skills across the primary age range.**
  What approaches to long-, medium- and short-term planning have you encountered in your placement schools? To what extent do your experiences of these align with the models of planning you have looked at in this chapter? What are the similarities or differences?

- **Become familiar with how to identify opportunities for planning computational thinking and coding as a subject in its own right and within other curriculum areas.**
  How has the computing PoS been adopted by your school? What strategies and approaches are used? Is computing taught discretely or embedded in subject schemes of work? What evidence do you have that this approach is/is not effective and why?

- **Identified potential opportunities to use specific programs or technology as well as unplugged activities to support the teaching of computational thinking and coding.**
  How has (a) the year group(s) you have taught in, and (b) the resources in the school(s) shaped or determined the way you have planned to teach computational thinking and coding?

Further resources and reading

Computing at School CAS community page. A hugely useful resource with searchable content for everything to do with teaching the computing curriculum. You need to register and once you do can subscribe to various email digests such as events and discussions:

http://community.computingatschool.org.uk/

(accessed 17 February 2017).

11 Assessing Pupil Progress in Computational Thinking and Coding

Learning outcomes

By the end of this chapter, you will:

- be familiar with some of the principal focuses of assessment;
- identify with the current national curriculum assessment needs for computing;
- review existing computing assessment approaches;
- develop ideas for assessing pupils' progress in computing, computational thinking and coding;
- understand how to accurately track the progress of your pupils in their computing-focused lessons.

Teachers' Standards

A teacher must:

1. Set high expectations which inspire, motivate and challenge pupils:

- set goals that stretch and challenge pupils of all backgrounds, abilities and dispositions.

2. Promote good progress and outcomes by pupils:

- be accountable for attainment, progress and outcomes of the pupils;
- plan teaching to build on pupils' capabilities and prior knowledge;
- guide pupils to reflect on the progress they have made and their emerging needs.

5. Adapt teaching to respond to the strengths and needs of all pupils:

- have a secure understanding of how a range of factors can inhibit pupils' ability to learn, and how best to overcome these;
- have a clear understanding of the needs of all pupils, and be able to use and evaluate distinctive teaching approaches to engage and support them.

6. Make accurate and productive use of assessment:

- know and understand how to assess the relevant subject and curriculum areas, including statutory assessment requirements;

(Continued)

> *(Continued)*
>
> - make use of formative and summative assessment to secure pupils' progress;
> - use relevant data to monitor progress, set targets, and plan subsequent lessons;
> - give pupils regular feedback, both orally and through accurate marking, and encourage pupils to respond to the feedback.
>
> (DfE, 2011)

Introduction

The purpose of this chapter is to explore existing practices in place for assessing pupil progress in computing. It will also propose possible assessment approaches that you might consider adopting in your computing classroom.

Assessment is at the heart of what teachers do in supporting their pupils' ability to progress within their subject.

Activity: why assess?

List as many different reasons you can think of as to why teachers assess pupils' work.

Compare your answers with those at the end of this chapter.

Assessment is an essential component of teacher planning and preparation. It needs to be appropriately and formally embedded in lessons and sequences of lessons. Alongside the significance of assessment in a child's learning, it is important to be mindful of its impact on the pupil. Assessment practices adopted by you need to be evaluated for their fitness to meet the assessment purpose and benefit required for the pupil. Are reliable and valid assessment choices being made? Assessment can be demotivating and have the opposite effect to many of the points you raised as a result of the activity above. With this in mind, it is imperative that teachers think very carefully about the assessment pedagogy choices they make, whether they will achieve what is wanted and the impact and value of these choices on the pupils and their progress.

What are you actually assessing in computing?

General methods and strategies for assessment are outside the scope of this book. If you require additional information about this, then further reading can be found towards the end of this chapter. The purpose of this section is to outline what needs to be assessed in the computing national curriculum.

Essentially, the formal assessment requirements in England are documented in the computing programmes of study (DfE, 2013) and contained within the Attainment Target (see KS1 and KS2 lists below). From a computational thinking and coding perspective the national curriculum (DfE, 2013a) clearly states that pupils must:

- Understand and apply the principles and concepts of computer science, including abstraction, logic, algorithms and data representation – *these are clearly framed with the concept of 'computational thinking'.*

- Analyse problems in computational terms, and have repeated practical experience of writing computer programs in order to solve such problems.

Computing programmes of study KS1 and KS2

Key Stage 1
Pupils should be taught to:

- *understand what algorithms are, how they are implemented as programs on digital devices, and that programs execute by following precise and unambiguous instructions;*
- *create and debug simple programs;*
- *use logical reasoning to predict the behaviour of simple programs;*
- use technology purposefully to create, organise, store, manipulate and retrieve digital content;
- recognise common uses of information technology beyond school;
- use technology safely and respectfully, keeping personal information private; identify where to go for help and support when they have concerns about content or contact on the internet or other online technologies.

Key Stage 2
Pupils should be taught to:

- *design, write and debug programs that accomplish specific goals, including controlling or simulating physical systems; solve problems by decomposing them into smaller parts;*
- *use sequence, selection, and repetition in programs; work with variables and various forms of input and output;*
- *use logical reasoning to explain how some simple algorithms work and to detect and correct errors in algorithms and programs;*
- understand computer networks, including the internet; how they can provide multiple services, such as the world wide web, and the opportunities they offer for communication and collaboration;

- use search technologies effectively, appreciate how results are selected and ranked, and be discerning in evaluating digital content;

- select, use and combine a variety of software (including internet services) on a range of digital devices to design and create a range of programs, systems and content that accomplish given goals, including collecting, analysing, evaluating and presenting data and information;

- use technology safely, respectfully and responsibly; recognise acceptable/unacceptable behaviour; identify a range of ways to report concerns about content and contact.

(DfE, 2013a)

This represents the minimum expectation required to be learned, and therefore assessed. Depending on the teacher level of expertise, a broader and deeper curriculum can of course be designed and offered. The *italicised* descriptors (above) refer directly to the science of computational thinking and will form the basis of learning and assessment within the class. It is important to view these descriptors holistically, and deliver computing-focused projects that broadly integrate what pupils should be taught. For example, a Year 6 project involving the design of a simple game using the *Scratch* programming platform will easily allow for the assessment of all of the following:

- design, write and debug programs that accomplish specific goals, including controlling or simulating physical systems; solve problems by decomposing them into smaller parts;

- use sequence, selection, and repetition in programs; work with variables and various forms of input and output;

- use logical reasoning to explain how some simple algorithms work and to detect and correct errors in algorithms and programs;

- select, use and combine a variety of software (including internet services) on a range of digital devices to design and create a range of programs, systems and content that accomplish given goals, including collecting, analysing, evaluating and presenting data and information;

- use technology safely, respectfully and responsibly; recognise acceptable/unacceptable behaviour; identify a range of ways to report concerns about content and contact.

It is, therefore, advisable to plan carefully to ensure the *Scratch* series of lessons will provide the learning opportunities to meet these descriptors and outcomes, and of course to assess the pupils' progress within them.

Potential approaches to engaging with and assessing computing progress

Schools are free to develop their own approaches to assessment that supports pupil progress and attainment (DfE, 2015). With this freedom to innovate assessment practice in mind, you might like to consider the following ideas we have seen being used effectively in schools:

Progression ladders/rubrics:

Use well-crafted learning objectives and carefully chosen assessment success criteria, using the national curriculum programmes of study. For each year group and/or key stage, a computing progression ladder is developed that articulates what learning must be demonstrated to move up 'the ladder' at *below*, *secure* or *exceeded* age-related expectations.

Evidence sheets/ workbooks/ progress passports:

Showing progress outcomes (formative and summative) and feedback including teacher and self/peer review commentary. This approach provides a very clear individual pupil log of work evidence, progress made, outcomes and their breadth and depth of understanding.

Mastery approach:

The mastery approach looks to ensure fundamental subject skills and concepts are considered in depth first before approaching the curriculum in a highly-structured and 'stepped' way. It aims to challenge and progress pupils' depth of understanding and fluency in the subject studied before any assessment credit is awarded (Kazu *et al.*, 2005). In order to progress, each 'step' must be mastered and progression to the next 'step' cannot be made until the pupil is assessed as secure in the stage they are currently working in. If a pupil is seen to be struggling to move to the next stage, then individual focused support and intervention can be applied to help the progress. Mastery should be viewed as the way the pupil has demonstrated a security of knowledge and understanding within wider computational concepts that are transferable between programming platforms for example.

> ## Research focus: a mastery approach to learning and assessment
>
> Lalley and Gentile in their 2009 article, *Classroom Assessment and Grading to Assure Mastery*, suggest a good mastery learning curriculum should incorporate the following:
>
> ⟶

1. *clearly stated and published objectives, sequenced to facilitate transfer of prior learning to current and future competencies;*

2. *a standard for passing mastery tests sufficiently high (e.g. 75% correct or better) to assure that initial learning, once forgotten (as is almost inevitable) can be relearned quickly;*

3. *multiple and parallel forms of criterion-referenced tests, with corrective exercises and retesting as needed to demonstrate initial mastery; and*

4. *grading incentives to encourage students to reach beyond initial mastery and strive for fluency in the material, to better organize, apply, and even teach it to others.*

(Lalley and Gentile, 2009, p.31)

Assessment in the EYFS

The computing programmes of study are neither statutory nor seen to be readily applicable in the EYFS. However, schemes of work do exist which both map the computing strands and reflect the teaching of computing and computational thinking skills to 3–5 year olds. How teachers go about assessing their pupils and the strategies they use, however, will vary to those you may see in Key Stages 1 and 2.

Ongoing daily formative assessments are *at the heart* of effective early years practice (BAECE, 2012, p.3). Observation as an assessment strategy therefore plays a vital role as children engage with and explore their environment. Given their peripatetic nature, young children are not often still for long periods of time. What they say and do as they interact with other people and engage with planned or free-flow activities may be written down by practitioners on sticky notes, or captured using a digital camera. This evidence, as well as any work they produce, will often be annotated to identify what they can do and inform planning future learning experiences and opportunities.

In line with assessment practice elsewhere in the primary phase, pupil progress is judged as being 'expected', 'emerging' or 'exceeding'. How a child's progress in computing and computational thinking is assessed will most likely – but not always – be determined by matching observations or other evidence against the 'prime' area of communication and language, as well as the 'specific' areas of literacy, mathematics, and understanding the world (as given in the examples in Chapter 10). If your school placement is in the EYFS then you may find that the most scope will come from evidencing the ways children demonstrate the three characteristics of effective learning:

- **playing and exploring** – children investigate and experience things, and 'have a go';
- **active learning** – children concentrate and keep on trying if they encounter difficulties, and enjoy achievements; and

- **creating and thinking critically** – children have and develop their own ideas, make links between ideas, and develop strategies for doing things.

(DfE, 2016, p.9)

Evidencing these characteristics can be particularly powerful because they can provide significant details about each child's learning and development and readily lend themselves to some of the concepts and approaches to computational thinking (CAS Barefoot Computing, 2014).

Activity: assessment in the EYFS

For each of the three characteristics of effective teaching and learning above identify the relevant early learning goals from the framework for the EYFS (DfE, 2014) and the computational thinking concepts and/or approaches (CAS Barefoot Computing, 2014) that you think match.

Now, have a look at the two examples of assessment evidence below and complete the rest of the grid.

Table 11.1   Assessment evidence grid

Evidence	Characteristic	Area of learning	ELG descriptor	CT concept/ approach
J is in the home corner which has been fashioned into a kitchen/café. She is putting items of plastic food onto plates. When asked what she is doing she says: 'I'm getting dinner ready for the three bears.'				
T is playing with a floor robot but the robot meets an obstacle. T stays where he is. E passes and stops, picks up the robot and repositions it so the path is clear then she walks away.				

Finally, as a means of recording summative assessment of attainment in computing in the EYFS, Gary Setchell (CAS Community) provides a spreadsheet to accomplish this using a colour-coded system to map the 'expected', 'emerging' or 'exceeding' descriptors and variations of them **http://community.computingatschool.org.uk/resources/2704**

Other suggested computing assessment options

Assessment is not just about recording attainment outcomes and grades. Although this is of essential importance, it represents *assessment of progress* and not *assessment for progress*. The latter is arguably the central constituent in ensuring the pupils achieve and attain what is expected of them. Building on the notion that 'one size does not fit all', this section will offer some further ideas that could be used to support the assessment of your pupils in progressing their learning within computing and computational thinking lessons.

'It's the learning not the doing': when assessing the pupils' progress, it is essential that the teacher considers what they have *learned* and not simply what they have *done*. The pupils have to *do* to *learn* but using assessment approaches that focus only on 'ticking off' what they have done is detrimental to understanding progress and is not effective assessment. Engaging with pupil understanding of computational thinking and the programming concepts they have chosen to employ is key in ascertaining the actual progress being made and therefore the next steps required.

Activity: assessment statements

Consider the statements below and identify what would constitute appropriate assessment opportunities and what might not. Compare your answers with those found at the end of this chapter.

Table 11.2 Assessment statements

I have included two sprites in my Scratch programme	I have explained how I have debugged my programme
I can effectively identify a problem and create a workable solution	I have completed three tasks
I can document the design processes and am able to discuss choices made	I have programmed six instructions
I have completed 20 lines of code to develop my solution	I know what an algorithm is
I have demonstrated resilience, learnt from the mistakes I have made and can explain where this has happened and why	I have evidenced sequence, selection and repetition in my programme

'Bloomify the approach'

Formulate your assessment to be appropriately tiered in outcome and expectation using Bloom's taxonomy (Bloom *et al.*,1956) – from assessing *knowledge and understanding* through to *evaluation and synthesis*. Or make use of the revised version created by Anderson *et al.*, (2001) and look to differentiate assessment from *remembering* through to *creating*. Assess the pupils' ability to recall programming terminology, facts and concepts but level assessment to also gauge and track their ability to understand, apply, analyse, evaluate and create within a programming domain. If you are unfamiliar with Bloom's work then visit **www. bloomstaxonomy.org/** for further information.

'Paired programming equals peer assessment'

Paired programming (see Chapter 4) is a technique that sees two pupils creating a programme at one computer. It is a well-rehearsed way of learning to program and code. One pupil is writing the code required while the other is checking the syntax as it is inputted. This in itself offers the clear chance of peer review – a common approach to assessment (e.g. Søndergaard and Mulder, 2012; Wang et al., 2015); but it could also be married with the following assessment opportunities when applicable: a group discussion and exchange of knowledge; peer marking of each other's work; and feedback with pupils correcting each other's work and reflecting on what could be done to improve it (Sitthiworachart and Joy, 2004). It is not an easy option, though, as it requires the pupil to have knowledge of the programming content they are looking to assess, as well as knowledge of the assessment processes needing to be applied. Pupils must have an understanding of the role they are undertaking in the process and see the value of it. Therefore, peer assessment and paired programming approaches have to be carefully planned for and embedded in lesson(s) for it to offer some dependability in supporting the progress of the pupils.

'Gamify the assessment'

Chapter 8 considers the use of gamification as a possible pedagogy for underpinning computational thinking learning. Gamification can also be used as a tool to support assessment and develop motivation in this area – particularly with formative approaches and the immediacy and fundamental need for feedback. Digital badges and rewards are utilised according to progress being made. Using quizzes such as 'Who Wants to be a Millionaire?' or the digital tool Kahoot also offers gamified approaches to the formative assessment and immediate feedback for the pupils (Fotaris et al., 2016). Using points as rewards in activity is a basic interpretation of gamification and assessment (Attali and Arieli-Attali, 2015) that could easily be applied in the classroom. Adopting different pathways through an activity (and therefore the assessment of it) can also exemplify gamified assessment. As with all assessment approaches however, gamifying it will require careful planning and thought. If this attention is taken then adopting gamified assessment strategy (perhaps coupled with gamified approaches to learning) provides the potential for increased pupil engagement in their assessment as well as enhanced formative feedback.

'Think technology'

If resources allow, then digitising assessment creates pupil excitement, intrigue and engagement in their assessment and saves the teacher time in recording the outcomes.

Online tools are now freely available to support this and are accessible across various computer and mobile platforms. Five of these tools worth exploring are: Kahoot (available here **https://getkahoot.com/**), Socrative (**https: //www.socrative.com/**), Padlet (**https:// padlet.com/**), Answer Garden (**https://answergarden.ch/**) and ClassDojo (**https://www. classdojo.com/en-gb**).

'Pupils diagnose the problems and set their goals'

This is rooted in a similar approach and reasoning as peer review. It is influenced by both *ipsative* and *diagnostic* assessment methodology. As with peer review, self-assessing learning encourages ownership and independence in the learning process. Self-assessment and self-diagnosis of problems being faced, fosters improved confidence, competence and proficiency in programming concepts. It deepens the learning experience and outcome for pupils, reinforces the notion of computational thinking and encourages the need for syntax error checking in the programmes they create.

'The pupil is the teacher'

Teachers need to be open to learning from their pupils (see Chapter 5). Pupils also need opportunities to verbalise and discuss their learning and understanding of the programs and algorithms they are writing. Peer teaching is a well-established and successful pedagogy in establishing learning and retention of knowledge. Using the pupil to teach their teacher (or peers) how they have developed their algorithm and/or program would be a good way of assessing the progress they are making within the curriculum. The pupil would have to demonstrate and articulate the way they are solving the 'problem', how they have applied computational thinking and logical reasoning, the inputs used, and the variables they have embedded and why. What is presented by the pupil provides a clear opportunity to assess progress either formatively or summatively. Having the pupil 'teach the teacher' may also help you if you are just beginning to familiarise yourself with the computing national curriculum.

'Use coding logs'

Encouraging the pupils to keep annotated logs, diaries or journals of the code using and the programming choices they are making, supports teacher assessment opportunity. They document clear evidence of pupil progress within their programming learning journey. Checklists can be used as part of this process but only if they evidence learning and not just what the pupils have 'done' or 'completed' in their coding activities. For example, the checklist should focus on the understanding of the programming principles used by the pupil and the reasons behind the choices made.

'Unplug the assessment'

The pupils' ability to think computationally and use logical reasoning can be assessed without the need for computers. Setting a paper-based activity where they 'program' each other to complete a set task will provide opportunities to assess their computational thinking capability. Creating an algorithm or set of 'move' instructions to develop a shape or diagram, which can be replicated on graph paper (for example) by a peer, would also demonstrate their skill base. Giving pupils 'cards' with various programming functions on and then providing them with some code that needs correcting using the cards is an excellent visual way of seeing who has understood and who has not. Why not use the medium of dance to teach and assess algorithmic understanding in a way that engages the pupils in a fun and exciting way?

'Authenticate the assessment'

Authentic assessment is a method that requires the pupils to perform 'real world' activities designed to test the skills and capabilities they have acquired. It promotes the application of programming skills rather than just the recall and comprehension of the concepts. For example, in developing the role of 'expert programmer' or 'expert game designer' the teacher plans and aims to assess pupils through:

- Interviewing for roles in their games design team;
- Creating and presenting their project plan;
- Briefing each other at the beginning of each lesson to suggest what will be created;
- Emailing, or otherwise entertaining a dialogue with their teacher each lesson for further feedback and goal setting;
- Group programming a solution – incorporating various assessment options;
- Presenting and justifying choices made, and solution programmed.

'Create a concept map'

Create a concept map that demonstrates the knowledge and understanding behind the computational 'problem' the pupils are solving and the perceived relationships between the different programming components and concepts they have included in the solutions created. This can be unplugged and hand drawn using pictures, cartoons and written text. It can be also be completed using various computer software platforms, or simply by an infographic including screenshots of what has been created, where and why.

'Use technical interviews'

NAACE (The Education Technology Association) suggest that the use of open-ended discussions or interviews is a good way to get the pupils to discuss their approaches to solving the problem they have been working on. These 'interviews' can be between peers and/or teachers. They should adopt open-ended, discursive questions that explore the choices the pupils have made and allows for the opportunity to justify the decisions made.

Activity: assessment opportunities

How might you look to embed effective assessment opportunities in your computing lessons? Which approaches will you use? Why? When? How will you judge your pupils' successes? What assessment strategies may be suitable for Early Years, KS1 or KS2?

Recording the computing assessments made:

This section considers how teacher assessment of the computing curriculum may be effectively documented. Assessments need to be recorded to allow the teacher to clearly articulate and evidence the progress being made by their pupils. Using data:

- provides opportunities for easier and more accurate pupil target setting; makes it easier to intervene with underachievers and locate when and where this is happening;

- enables all those in the school community who need to understand the progress being made by the pupils;

- involves parents in the learning of their children – think how tracked data can help with parents' evenings, for example;

- provides accessible, accurate information for planning lessons;

- evidences a clear picture of the individual pupil's attainment;

- presents a clear(er) picture to the pupil during the lesson(s) and the opportunity to discuss their progress and set appropriate formative goals;

- provides a means of recording observations made of progress during a lesson(or lessons);

- allows for far greater efficiency and effectiveness in analysis of progress/ achievement/ attainment;

- provides accurate transitional data between KS2 and KS3 (see Chapter 12).

Activity: tracking progress

As you move into your school-based placements, explore how your school is recording computing progress and tracking data. Create a data tracker for your class using appropriate computer software, which will enable you to intervene with and evidence your pupils' progress in computing.

Here we have considered ways in which you can formally record your pupil assessments. For methods that can be used to informally note this progress, perhaps consider this website as a starting point:

www.education.com/reference/article/informal-methods-assessment/

Assessment list from the activity on p.155

- Find out what has been learned;
- Grade some work and ensure appropriate standards are being met;
- Gather accurate objective and subjective data on the pupil's progress and level of understanding;
- Compare outcomes within the class, school and with other institutions;
- Improve the pupil's learning;
- Inform planning;
- See if learning outcomes have been achieved;
- Let pupils know where they are, and how they can improve;
- Set targets for our pupils;
- Motivate and encourage pupils;
- Find out what pupils can do;
- Gauge what is understood;
- Scrutinise our teaching successes.

Table of assessment statements from the activity on p.161

Table 11.3 Assessment statements from activity

Appropriate assessment approach?	Not appropriate?
I have explained how I have debugged my program	I have included two sprites in my Scratch program
I can effectively identify a problem and create a workable solution	I have completed three tasks
I can document the design processes and am able to discuss choices made	I have programmed six instructions
I have demonstrated resilience, learned from the mistakes I have made and can explain where this has happened and why	I have completed 20 lines of code to develop my solution
	I know what an algorithm is
	I have evidenced sequence, selection and repetition in my program

Learning outcomes review

By engaging with this chapter you are now in a position to challenge yourself to adequately assess your pupils' computing progress. You will have reflected on various approaches that could be used to assess your pupils' progress as well as considering how these assessments could be adequately tracked and evidenced.

Within the context of your school-based placements, consider the following questions in reviewing your knowledge and understanding of the content covered in this chapter:

- **Be familiar with some of the principal focuses of assessment.**
  List all the methods you have used to assess your pupils. Which techniques have proved most successful in promoting progress and/or identifying outcomes? Why?

- **Identify with the current national curriculum assessment needs for computing.**
  How does the programme of study translate itself into the classroom? What steps are your placement schools taking to ensure adequate coverage of computing learning? What are the implications for practitioners in the EYFS? What steps are you taking?

- **Review existing computing assessment approaches.**
  Are the approaches discussed in this chapter being adopted in your placement schools? What successes/ problems are you and your colleagues facing in assessing pupil progress in computing?

- **Develop ideas for assessing pupils' progress in computing, computational thinking and coding.**
  Have you embraced some of the computing assessment suggestions provided in this chapter? What assessment ideas have you developed? What pros and cons can be identified in what you have used?

- **Understand how to accurately track the progress of your pupils in their computing-focused lessons.**
  Review the computing assessment tracker you have created. How have you used it to identify and intervene with your pupils' progress? What improvements will you now be making in how you effectively track the outcomes and progress of your pupils?

Further reading and resources

Department for Education (DfE) (2013) *'National Curriculum in England: Computing programmes of study'.* Crown Copyright.

Will allow you to further engage with English National Curriculum content and therefore what capabilities pupils are being assessed against across the key stages.

Computing at School (CAS) (2015) *'QuickStart Computing: A CPD Toolkit for secondary teachers'*. Pp.12–17. Although a secondary phase publication, Progression Pathways assessment model information is documented here.

Lalley, J and Gentile, JR (2009) Classroom Assessment and Grading to Assure Mastery, *Theory Into Practice*, 48(1): 28–35.

If you are considering mastery approaches, then this article is a good starting point.

Black, P and Wiliam, D (1998) *Inside the Black Box: Raising standards through classroom assessment*. London: Granada Learning.

A highly significant publication considering the impact of formative assessment in the classroom.

Cremin, T and Arthur, J (eds.) (2010) *Learning to Teach in the Primary School.* UK: Routledge.

Read Section 5, Assessment, pp.311–339, for further information regarding general assessment method and strategy.

Standards and Testing Agency (STA) (2016) *2017 Assessment and Reporting Arrangements (ARA) October 2016.* London.

This guidance provided by the STA details the statutory requirements for the Early Years Foundation Stage (EYFS) profile assessment and reporting for the 2016 to 2017 academic year.

12 Transition Issues: Bridging the Computing Gap between KS2 and KS3

Learning outcomes

By the end of this chapter, you will:

- develop an understanding of the complexities involved in Key Stage 2 (KS2) to Key Stage 3 (KS3) transition;
- reflect on some potential strategies designed to support KS2 to KS3 computing transition;
- review existing transition approaches being used by your placement schools.

Teachers' Standards

A teacher must:

2. Promote good progress and outcomes by pupils:

- be accountable for attainment, progress and outcomes of the pupils;
- plan teaching to build on pupils' capabilities and prior knowledge.

3. Demonstrate good subject and curriculum knowledge:

- have a secure knowledge of the relevant subject(s) and curriculum areas, foster and maintain pupils' interest in the subject, and address misunderstandings.

4. Plan and teach well-structured lessons:

- promote a love of learning and children's intellectual curiosity;
- set homework and plan other out-of-class activities to consolidate and extend the knowledge and understanding pupils have acquired;
- contribute to the design and provision of an engaging curriculum within the relevant subject area(s).

5. Adapt teaching to respond to the strengths and needs of all pupils:

- have a clear understanding of the needs of all pupils, and be able to use and evaluate distinctive teaching approaches to engage and support them.

6. Make accurate and productive use of assessment:

- use relevant data to monitor progress, set targets, and plan subsequent lessons.

(DfE, 2011)

Introduction

Primary to secondary phase transition represents a daunting prospect for many pupils and their parents. It also offers numerous complexities for secondary school computing teachers and subject leaders.

Pupils will need to adjust from being the oldest in the school to being the youngest. They will be mixing with a lot of unfamiliar children and having to form new relationships and friendships. They will be placed in subject-based classes that they will have to move around the school to attend. They will most likely be placed in sets in a number of subjects or streamed by ability. Their workload will probably increase. From a secondary curriculum subject perspective, transition in computing is often awkward. Pupils will arrive from a diverse assortment of primary feeder schools, with a varying level of computing skill. Depending on the skillset of teachers in these primary schools and the curriculum time available, some pupils will have experienced programming, for example, and will have been exposed to a progressive computing primary curriculum. Others may have concentrated more on the digital literacy aspect of using multimedia presentation software or creating simple spreadsheets. This makes planning for the beginnings of a Key Stage 3 (KS3) computing curriculum very challenging. Secondary school computing subject leaders and teachers are rarely able to build an accurate progress picture of their incoming pupils beyond what their maths and English capability looks like.

There are therefore clear challenges if pupils are to be confident and continue progressing their computing learning, attainment and enjoyment as they move into the secondary school environment. This chapter will consider some of these challenges and offer some potential strategies for supporting effective computing curriculum transition between Key Stage 2 and Key Stage 3.

Activity: reflecting on your own experience

Think back to your own transition experience when you were at school.

What issues did you face? What issues do you think your teachers faced?

How could transition have been improved for you?

How could the teachers ensure the smooth transition of specific subjects from primary school to secondary school?

The following case study briefly discusses outcomes from some school computing curriculum transition action research conducted by a trainee teacher.

Case study: transition action research

During her initial teacher training and education, Sheharbano undertook an action research inquiry looking at pupil computing skills at the point of primary to secondary transition. She had identified the problem of pupils arriving at secondary school without any clear confidence or competence in many fundamentals of the computing curriculum and looked to create appropriate interventions to 'bridge this gap' in capability. The research was conducted in a school in east London that is in the bottom eight of the London Poverty Profile of 2015, and as such suggests a high proportion of disadvantaged pupils attend the school – so additional intervention was likely to be required as an appropriate strategy for raising pupil achievement and outcomes. Interventions were agreed with her deputy head teacher, and a sample of pupils from Years 5 and 6 in a selected primary school were chosen to form a 'computing club'. Over a number of weeks, Sheharbano used this club to measure the pupils' current computing capability and form the interventions she wished to use to bridge gaps found. Interventions were designed with gamification underpinnings (see Chapter 8) using characters, missions and an adventure quest to strengthen the learning approach and seek pupil engagement and motivation. Initial findings suggested these interventions had a positive and noticeable impact on the pupils' progress in the competencies and capability needed to successfully transition into a KS3 computing curriculum. Sheharbano's study identified the following additional targets the school could consider in helping to ensure smooth computing curriculum continuity into the secondary phase of education:

1. Engage with local secondary school computing departments to receive input into computing needs. Her interviews with primary colleagues suggested they had very little confidence to teach the primary computing curriculum.

2. Increase computing curriculum time (in the selected primary school) to at least one hour a week to help support the necessary skills required to develop competency in computing.

3. Ask secondary school computing colleagues to provide a checklist of what they would like covered in Year 6 (as a starting point).

4. The 'harder' aspects of the curriculum should not be ignored in favour of digital literacy and ICT activities. Whereas these are important areas and should not be disregarded, the computer science element of the curriculum must also be engaged with.

Sheharbano's case study therefore suggests, that in many primary schools, pupils may not be ready to effectively progress their computing understanding at a fitting 'level' in moving into KS3. To combat this, suitable intervention strategies need to be implemented to ensure appropriate and expected curriculum continuity.

Potential strategies to help bridge a computing gap

This section proposes some ideas that schools use/could use in helping to bridge the transitional gap between primary and secondary school computing. Traditionally it is left to the secondary school and its feeder primary schools to decide how to best work transition for the pupils. This commonly sees secondary schools run open days/evenings, induction days, parents' evenings, parents' meetings and create information brochures and prospectuses for parents and pupils. Year 7 teachers will often visit primary feeder schools to give talks and lessons about the secondary school the pupils will be attending, and the routines and expectations that are in place. This helps ensure that the emotional facets of transition that pupils face are appropriately engaged with, something that has been historically concentrated on during the transition phase (Ofsted, 2002).

Successful transition does, however, also need to ensure curriculum continuity (Galton *et al.,* 2000; DfES, 2004; Evangelou *et al.,* 2008). Curriculum continuity should involve teachers and pupils in projects that start in Year 6 and are completed in Year 7 in the secondary school the pupils move into (Galton *et al.*, 1999), and thus offering some consistency of teaching approaches and subject content being engaged with. It is an area that has received considerable government focus in recent years (see Curriculum Continuity: Effective transfer between primary and secondary schools; DfES, 2004) in an attempt to support pupil progress during the awkward transition phase, and move them forward at an appropriate pace. Pupil progress is often hindered during this transition phase in a child's education (Galton *et al.*, 2000; Evangelou *et al.*, 2008) and 'learning loss' can manifest itself. This suggests clearly it is imperative that collaborative involvement between primary and secondary colleagues in developing a continuous Key Stage 1 to 3 computing curriculum needs consideration.

Research focus: what makes for successful transition?

Evangelou *et al.* (2008) present findings of a study of over 500 children, into what makes for successful transition. The report suggests five things are required for transition to work effectively. These are:

- The opportunity for pupils to develop their confidence by making new friends and relationships;

- Parents have no concerns because their child has settled into their new school appropriately;

- Pupils are showing clear interest and engagement in their new school work;

- Pupils understand the new routines expected of them;

- Curriculum continuity takes place.

→

> Most children, but not all, suggested that the transition processes worked for them. The study also clearly found that curriculum continuity was a vital component for effective transition and was required to help foster clear pupil interest in their school, their learning and their inevitable progress.

To support this need for effective computing curriculum continuity, you might like to consider the following suggestions:

1. *Seek computing CPD support from your secondary partner schools*: within computing, successful curriculum transition will require confidence in the primary teacher in delivering their computing-focused lessons. One way of supporting this is to seek CPD support from your secondary computing teacher colleagues. Secondary phase Initial Teacher Training (ITT) courses are currently geared to develop computer science teachers and most schools are now also offering a GCSE in the subject as it counts in the English Baccalaureate (EBacc). There is blossoming expertise in your secondary partner schools that could (and perhaps should) be engaged with in supporting the development of your skillset and capability in creating and delivering a valuable primary computing curriculum offer. This approach is supportive of Evangelou's transition research findings in that it will help provide a better understanding for teachers of the differences in teaching between primary and secondary phase. It will also allow parents to see schools better preparing their children for the work required in their secondary school (Evangelou *et al.*, 2008).

2. *Partner with other local primary schools*: in order for teachers to develop the critical thinking skills required to become 'agents of change' during their pre-service training and beyond (Price and Valli, 2005; Braund and Campbell, 2009; Marchel *et al.*, 2011; MacPhail and Tannehill, 2012), one important approach for effective change and reinvention is to work collaboratively in conjunction with colleagues in other local primary schools in supporting this transformation. Collaborating with your colleagues in local primary schools, writing and creating a Key Stage 1 and 2 computing curriculum together, and supporting each other in delivering it, would seem a worthwhile activity to engage in. Consistency of the curriculum in feeder schools will only enhance computing continuity into the secondary phase of the pupils' schooling.

3. *Create coding transition projects*: drawing on the curriculum transition and continuity research of Galton *et al.* (1999), creating coding and computing projects that can start in the summer term of Year 6 and be completed in the autumn term of Year 7 is a meaningful venture. These 'bridging projects' would normally be taught by primary teachers in Year 6 and handed over to secondary computing teachers for the beginning of Year 7 (Powell *et al.*, 2006). The projects would facilitate talk between secondary computing departments and their feeder school colleagues. They would see a consensus

arrived at in pedagogy and approaches to teaching computing, as well as agreement of assessment and standards expected to be reached. They will certainly offer continuity of the computing curriculum from the latter stages of the pupil's primary schooling through to the early stages of the secondary phase.

4. *Plan the KS2 and KS3 computing curriculum together*: Secondary and primary teacher colleagues plan the work together. This encourages conformity of content, activity, pedagogy, assessment, standards and CPD needs. Parents can be satisfied that their children are being adequately provided for in their computing transition and be comfortable that appropriate standards are being met in their learning across the two key stages. Assessment pathways and strategies (see Chapter 11) can be agreed and produced. Progress can be adequately mapped and exchanged between schools. This collaborative approach can be further enhanced by using technological tools that will allow for joint editing and contributing (e.g. Google Docs and Dropbox).

5. *Organise 'Computing Challenge Days'*: a quick search of the internet reveals that these are gaining in popularity. They often seem to form part of a wider celebration of curriculum achievement in a primary school. However, you could easily partner with your local primary and secondary school(s) and run a 'robot wars', 'games design', 'Raspberry Pi', 'code battle', 'ethical hacking' or 'mobile phone app' challenge. Secondary phase colleagues' experience and expertise can be drawn on in supporting these challenges as well as potentially using their facilities and pupils to help champion the event.

6. *Pass computing data and assessment information on to secondary colleagues*: Chapter 11 has provided ideas for potential ways of recording assessments made in primary computing lessons. Sharing this information with the secondary schools that your pupils will be attending is highly important in enabling them to tailor a curriculum that will appropriately continue and challenge learning in computing. It also affords the chance to discuss computing curricula choices and pupil outcomes with colleagues that could facilitate some of the other aspects of successful curriculum transition to occur.

7. *Summarise KS2 content for KS3 teachers prior to transition:* could (and should perhaps) accompany the sharing of assessed computing outcomes. Planning a Key Stage 2/ Key stage 3 computing curriculum together with secondary colleagues is not always a viable option. If this proves difficult, then providing a précis of Key Stage 2 topics covered and learning and teaching approaches taken to deliver this content, will allow the Year 7 computing teacher evidence that can ensure she/he is meeting the appropriate needs of their pupils.

8. *Team teach with secondary colleagues*: if transition and computing bridging projects are something that you consider valuable in supporting curriculum continuity from Year 6 to Year 7, then why not look to team teach them? Year 7 secondary computing teachers could help underpin the teaching in primary school during the summer term prior to

transition. If time and logistics permit, Year 6 teachers could also visit Year 7 computing classrooms in the autumn term following school change and support the bridging lessons taking place.

9. *Get the parents involved*: parental involvement and the home-life experiences of the pupil is key to their successful education and outcomes. With this in mind, let us briefly consider parental impact in school transition.

Research focus: parental impact on transition

There has been much research into the involvement and impact of parents in successful transitions from one education stage to another. Anderson *et al.* (2000) identify the following reasons as to why this is seen as important. They suggest parents involved in the transition processes are more likely to remain involved in their child's schooling as they transfer into the next stage of their education; parent participation tends to equate to pupil participation in transition and the motivation to do so; communication is enhanced between parents and their child's next stage teachers, ensuring early relationships are established and an easier approach to intervening if problems occur.

From a computing stance, it would also be useful to involve parents who work in the computing and information technology industry in the curricula or extra curricula computing activity being provided, in supporting curriculum transition between Key Stage 2 and Key Stage 3. This contact is supportive of parental involvement in transition processes. It is also accommodating industry and real world input into a fledgling curriculum, something that various bodies (eg. CAS, BCS) advocate.

Activity: involving parents

How are your schools using and supporting parents in the transitional phases? How would you like to use your pupils' parents to ensure the curriculum is suitably 'bridged' from Key Stage 2 to 3?

10. *Pupil mentoring*: research into pupil peer mentoring is prolific (eg. Quince and Layman, 2006; O'Hara, 2011; James *et al.*, 2014) and suggests that it can impact very positively on pupils' emotional literacy (O'Hara, 2011) in supporting the anxieties of moving school. However, it can also be argued that pupils could be used to help mentor their peers' curriculum learning continuity and outcome achievement. As part of a 'bridging the curriculum gap' approach, secondary school computing/computer science pupils could

support their Year 5 and 6 peers in primary computing lessons and transitional projects. Peer teaching as an assessment tool was discussed in Chapter 11. It could provide an excellent opportunity for both the 'teacher/mentor' and the 'pupil' to develop confidence, resilience and understanding in the computing fundamentals of the curriculum, as well as enhancing curriculum continuity successes.

11. *Summer School computing*: Summer schools are often in place to support disadvantaged or underachieving pupils in their transition from a primary to secondary school curriculum (Siddiqui *et al.*, 2014). Schools can fund these activities through their Pupil Premium allocation. It is a potential way of allowing these pupils to 'catch up' with their computing curriculum and bridge any perceived gaps in their confidence and learning. DfE funded research by Day *et al.* (2013) suggests summer schools can have a tangible impact on pupils by allowing for early intervention actions in advance of their first year at secondary school. In the quest to ensure successful computing curriculum transition, running a summer school for an interested primary intake may be a positive and worthwhile intervention.

12. *Computing masterclasses for high attainers and achievers*: gifted and talented provision in schools has been the subject of educational policy initiatives for many years (Tennant and Harries, 2012). Gifted and talented strategy and implementation in schools often takes the form of intervention through accelerated learning programmes and enriching the pupils' curriculum by exploring the breadth and depth of the subject in greater detail. Computing masterclasses will enable these gifted and talented facets to be offered. If the expertise exists at primary level then they could be run in this environment. If not, specialist extra-curricular groups can be brought in or, perhaps more applicably in supporting successful KS2 to KS3 curriculum transition, secondary computing teacher colleagues could lead these classes.

The case study below explores how a Primary with computing trainee has worked to improve curriculum continuity and transition in one of their placement schools.

Case study: supporting curriculum continuity

Oliver, a primary with computing trainee teacher, volunteered in his third school-based placement to implement some ideas for supporting and improving computing curriculum transition from Year 6 to Year 7. He could see that the computing provision in his training school currently lacked some appropriate breadth and depth of input due to the lack of computing expertise among the current staff members. Having spoken to some secondary phase computer science student teacher colleagues at his training institution, Oliver was concerned that his pupils may not be best equipped for their transition into a Year 7 computing environment.

→

To improve things and help enhance his pupils' computing expertise in readiness for their new school, Oliver implemented the following steps (with permission from his headteacher and leadership colleagues):

1. Contacted the local secondary school where most of his pupils would be attending, and arranged extra-curricula classes focusing on coding and algorithmic thinking. These classes were taught at the secondary school by colleagues in their computing department. The approach supported the emotional transitional issues that the pupils may have experienced as well as developed their curriculum understanding in preparation for their Key Stage 3 computing study.

2. The culmination of these classes was a celebration event at Oliver's training school. This took place one evening in the summer term and involved parents, primary school teachers and the secondary school colleagues who supported the delivery, in championing the pupils' work and outcomes. The secondary school headteacher attended and governors from both schools were invited. Oliver also invited local IT-focused businesses to be present. Pupils were asked to present their coded solutions in their classroom settings. Guest were able to interact with their work and ask questions about what each pupil had done and chosen to create. Overall 'winners' were selected and prizes awarded.

Oliver's input here helped him secure a permanent teaching position at his training school. He has developed excellent working relationships with his secondary school computing teacher colleagues. Currently Oliver is working to repeat this project but also to enhance curriculum continuity and transition in further ways. This is including writing a KS1 and 2 computing curriculum in association with his secondary phase colleagues to help ensure content covered at primary level is appropriate preparation for KS3. Oliver is also talking to other primary schools in his area to work on a collaborative 'feeder' school approach to computing and curriculum consistency.

Some of the successes of Oliver's approach are acknowledged below:

...we were only too happy to run additional after school classes in the summer term for Oliver's computing pupils. It meant we could get the children ready for the Year 7 computing curriculum we have in place, both in terms of subject understanding but also relationships and rapport needed to teach them. We have also started working more closely with our primary school colleagues which can only be good in supporting their progress into Key Stage 3.

Head of computing, Secondary School.

...the celebration evening was a fantastic event. I had no idea my daughter was so interested in computers and what makes them work. Her presentation and game (and those of her classmates) was excellent and I am extremely pleased to see her develop this digital skillset.

Parent, Year 6.

Activity: bridging the transition from KS2 to KS3

What are your placement schools doing to help bridge the transitional gap in computing?

What strategies are they implementing in association with the secondary school(s) they feed into?

What can you offer to support the transition strategy in place?

Learning outcomes review

This chapter has considered the complexities of pupils transitioning, within a computing curriculum, from Key Stage 2 to Key Stage 3. Transition is a complicated and often stressful experience for those involved and can have significant impact on a pupil's social and emotional adjustment as well as their continuing academic performance (Bailey and Baines, 2012). To enable you to reflect on your learning of the content in this chapter and assess your own progress against the intended learning outcomes, please reflect on the questions raised below:

- **Develop an understanding of the complexities involved in KS2 to KS3 transition.**
  Talk to your primary teacher colleagues during your school-based placements and find out what they perceive to be transitional complexities and barriers. How are they looking to overcome them in their practice? In their schools? Particularly in computing?
  What are Year 6 pupil opinions and worries regarding their movement from primary school to secondary school?

- **Reflect on some potential strategies designed to support KS2 to KS3 computing transition.**
  List the transitional and 'bridging the gap' strategies your placement schools use and evaluate the successes that are being achieved here. Are there any specific to computing? What successes and problems can be identified here? During your school placements, have you had an opportunity to assist and contribute with transition? If so, what was your involvement and how successful do you think it was in supporting effective transition and curriculum continuity? Rank the strategies in order of perceived impact and success for pupils, parents and the schools involved.

Further reading and resources

Anderson, LW, Jacobs, J, Schramm, S, Splittgerber, F (2000) School transitions: beginning of the end or a new beginning? *International Journal of Educational Research*, 33: 325–339.

An article that considers transitional stress theory and the child's own appraisal of their transition to secondary school.

Evangelou, M, Taggart, B, Sylva, K, Melhuish, E, Sammons, P and Sirai-Blatchford, I (2008) *What makes a successful transition from primary to secondary school.* Research Report DCSF-RR019. IOE: London.

An informative report into the complexities of transition and issues faced by pupils, schools, parents and local authorities.

Galton, M, Morrison, I, Pell, T (2000) Transfer and transition in English schools: reviewing the evidence, *International Journal of Educational Research*, 33: 341–363.

A significant study into the impact of school change and transition on pupil performance.

References

2Simple Ltd. (2016) *2Simple 2Code*. Available at: **www.2simple.com/2Code** (accessed 22 February 2017).

Al-Bow, M, Austin, D, Edgington, J, Fajardo, R, Fishburn, J, Lara, C, Leutenegger, S and Meyer, S (2009) *Using game creation for teaching computer programming to high school students and teachers*. Proceedings of the 14th annual ACM SIGCSE conference on Innovation and technology in computer science education. pp.104–108. New York: ACM.

Alexander, R (2008) *Towards Dialogic Teaching: rethinking classroom talk.* (4th ed.) York: Dialogos.

Anderson, LW, Jacobs, J, Schramm, S and Splittgerber, F (2000) School transitions: beginning of the end or a new beginning? *International Journal of Educational Research*, 33: 325–339

Anderson, LW, Krathwohl, DR, Airasian, PW, Cruikshank, KA, Mayer, RE, Pintrich, PR, Raths, J and Wittrock, MC (2001) *A Taxonomy for Learning, Teaching, and Assessing: A revision of Bloom's Taxonomy of Educational Objectives*. New York: Pearson, Allyn and Bacon.

Anderson, M (2013) *Students as Leaders*. **https://ictevangelist.com/students-as-leaders/** (accessed 17 February 2017).

Apps for Good (2015) *Apps for Good – Our Vision*. Available at: **www.appsforgood.org/** (accessed 17 February 2017).

AppShed Ltd. (2016) *App creation for education*. Available at: **https://appshed.com/** (accessed 17 February 2017).

Attali, Y and Arieli-Attali, M (2015) Gamification in assessment: Do points affect test performance? *Computers and Education*, 83: 57–63.

British Association for Early Childhood Education (BAECE) (2012) *Development Matters in the Early Years Foundation Stage (EYFS)*. Available at: **www.foundationyears.org.uk/ files/2012/03/Development-Matters-FINAL-PRINT-AMENDED.pdf** (accessed 17 February 2017).

Bagge, P (2015) *Eight steps to promote problem solving and resilience and combat learnt helplessness in computing*. Available at: **http://philbagge.blogspot.co.uk/2015/02/eight-steps-to-promote-problem-solving.html#comment-form** (accessed 17 February 2017).

Bailey, S, and Baines, E (2012) The impact of risk and resiliency factors on the adjustment of children after transition from primary to secondary school, *Educational and Child Psychology*, 29(1): 47–63.

Barr, D, Harrison, J and Conery, L (2011) Computational Thinking: A Digital Age Skill for Everyone. *International Society for Technology in Education*, March/April, pp.20–23.

Berners-Lee, T (2000) *Weaving the Web: The Original Design and Ultimate Destiny of the World Wide Web.* New York: Harper Collins.

Berry, M (2013a) *Froebel and the pedagogy of computing.* Available at: **http://milesberry. net/2013/09/froebel-and-the-pedagogy-of-computing/** (accessed 17 February 2017).

Berry, M (2013b) *Computing in the national curriculum: A guide for primary teachers.* Available at: **www.computingatschool.org.uk/data/uploads/CASPrimaryComputing.pdf** (accessed 17 February 2017).

Berry, M (2014) *Computational Thinking in Primary Schools.* Available at: **http://milesberry. net/2014/03/computational-thinking-in-primary-schools/** (accessed 17 February 2017).

Berry, M (2015) *Computing at School (CAS) Quick Start Computing - A CPD toolkit for Primary Teachers.* London: Department for Education.

Bers, M, Strawhacker, A, Lee, M and Caine, C (2015) *ScratchJr Demo: A coding language for Kindergarten,* Massachusetts: DevTech Research Group.

Bloom, BS (ed.), Engelhart, MD, Furst, EJ, Hill, WH, Krathwohl, DR (1956) *Taxonomy of Educational Objectives, Handbook I: The Cognitive Domain.* New York: David McKay Co Inc.

Boeijen, G, Kneepkens, B and Thijssen, J (2010) *Natuurkunde en techniek voor de basisschool, een domeinbeschrijving als resultaat van een cultuurpedagogische discussie (physics and technology for primary education).* Arnhem: Cito.

Braund, M and Campbell, B (2009) Learning to Teach About Ideas and Evidence in Science: The Student Teacher as Change Agent, *Research in Science Education,* 40: 203–222

Bray, B and McClaskey, K (2013) *Personalised Learning Chart (Version 3).* Available at: **http:// barbarabray.net/2012/01/22/personalization-vs-differentiation-vs-individualization-chart/** (accessed 17 February 2017).

British Computing Society (2007) *Computational Thinking.* Available at: **www.bcs.org/ content/conWebDoc/11837** (accessed 17 February 2017).

Bruner, J (1960) *The Process of Education* (2nd ed.). Cambridge: Harvard University Press.

Bruner, JS, Ross, G and Wood, DJ (1976) The role of tutoring in problem solving. *Journal of Child Psychiatry and Psychology,* 17(2): 89–100.

Caldwell, H and Bird, J (2015) *Teaching with tablets.* London: SAGE.

Carver, SM. and Klahr, D (1986) Assessing Children's Logo Debugging Skills with a Former Model, *Education Computing Research,* 2(4): 487–525.

CAS Barefoot Computing (2014) *Computational Thinking.* Available at: **http://barefootcas. org.uk/barefoot-primary-computing resources/concepts/computational-thinking/** (accessed 17 February 2017).

Computer Science Unplugged (2016) *CS Unplugged: Computer science without a computer.* Available at: **http://csunplugged.org/about/** (accessed 17 February 2017).

Condie, R and Munro, B with Seagraves, L and Kenesson, S (2007) *The Impact of ICT in Schools: A Landscape Review*. Coventry: Becta.

Csikszentmihalyi, M (1990) *Flow: The psychology of optimal experience*. New York: Harper Perennial.

Csizmadia, A, Curzon, P, Dorling, M, Humphreys, S, Ng, T, Selby, C and Woollard, J (2015) *Computational Thinking a Guide for Teachers*. London: Hodder Education.

Davidson, J (2015) *Here's How Many Internet Users There Are*, Time Magazine, 26 May. Available at: **http://time.com/money/3896219/internet-users-worldwide/** (accessed 17 February 2017).

Davies, R (2014) Computing, programming and pedagogy, *Computing at School Newsletter*, Autumn: 1–2. Available at: **www.computingatschool.org.uk/data/uploads/newsletter-autumn-2014.pdf** (accessed 17 February 2017).

Day, L, Martin, K, Sharp, C, Gardner, R, and Barham, J (2013) *Disadvantaged Pupils: Key findings for Schools Research report*. NFER and Ecorys.

Department for Education (DfE) (2011) *Teachers' standards*. London: DfE.

DfE (2013a) *National curriculum in England: Computing programmes of study: Key Stages 1 and 2*. London: DfE.

DfE (2013b) *National curriculum in England: Physical education programmes of study: Key Stages 1 and 2*. London: DfE.

DfE (2013c) *National curriculum in England: Mathematics programmes of study: Key Stages 1 and 2*. London: DfE.

DfE (2014) *Statutory framework for the early years foundation stage*. London: DfE.

DfE (2015) *Running a school: myths and facts*. Available at: **https://www.gov.uk/government/uploads/system/uploads/attachment_data/file/482564/Myths_and_facts.pdf** (accessed 17 February 2017).

DfE (2016) *Early years foundation stage profile 2017 Handbook*. London: DfE.

Department for Education and Employment (DfEE) (1999) *The National Curriculum: Handbook for Primary Teachers in England*. London: Qualification and Curriculum Authority (QCA) (2007) ICT Programme of Study and Attainment Target.

Department for Education and Skills (DfES) (2004) *Curriculum Continuity: Effective transfer between primary and secondary schools*. London: DfES.

Desailly, J (2012) *Creativity in the Primary Classroom*. London: SAGE.

Deterding, S, Dixon, D, Khaled, R and Nacke, L (2011) *From game design elements to gamefulness: Defining gamification*. Proceedings of the 15th international Academic Mindtrek Conference pp.9–15. ACM.

DevTech Research Group (2016) *About ScratchJr.* Available at: **https://www.scratchjr.org/about.html** (accessed 17 February 2017).

Digital Leader Network (2016) *Digital Leader Network: Collaborative Blogging Between Schools.* Available at: **www.digitalleadernetwork.co.uk/** (accessed 22 February 2017).

Dorling, M and Browning, P (2015) *CAS Computing Progression Pathways KS1 (Y1) to KS3 (Y9) by topic.* Available at: **http://community.computingatschool.org.uk/resources/1692** (accessed 17 February 2017).

Drew, R (2016) *UNICEF Rights Respecting School.* Available at: **http://geariesprimaryschool.blogspot.co.uk/2016/07/unicef-rights-respecting-school.html** (accessed 17 February 2017).

Dunne, E and Zandstra, R (2011) *Students as change agents – new ways of engaging with learning and teaching in higher education.* Bristol: A joint University of Exeter/ESCalate/ Higher Education Academy Publication. Available at: **http://escalate.ac.uk/8064** (accessed 17 February 2017).

Enabling Enterprise (2015) *Enabling Enterprise - Primary Schools.* Available at: **http://enablingenterprise.org/wp-content/uploads/2015/03/EE-Primary-School-Brochure-2015-vFinal.pdf** (accessed 17 February 2017).

Evangelou, M, Taggart, B, Sylva, K, Melhuish, E, Sammons, P and Sirai-Blatchford, I (2008) *What makes a successful transition from primary to secondary school.* Research Report DCSF-RR019. London: IOE.

Fotaris, P, Mastoras, T, Leinfellner, R, and Rosunally, Y (2016) Climbing Up the Leaderboard: An Empirical Study of Applying Gamification Techniques to a Computer Programming Class, *Electronic Journal of e-Learning,*14(2): 95–110.

Franklin, J (2016) *Tips for Effective Paired Programming.* Available at: **www.axsied.com/wp-content/uploads/2016/06/Effective-Pair-Programming-8.pdf** (accessed 17 February 2017).

Galton, M, Gray, J and Ruddock, J (1999) *The Impact of School Transitions and Transfers on Pupil Progress and Attainment.* London: DfEE.

Galton, M, Morrison, I and Pell, T (2000) Transfer and transition in English schools: reviewing the evidence, *International Journal of Educational Research*, 33: 341–363.

Gifford, C (2005) *Robots.* Haarlem: J.H. Gottmer.

Goode, J Chapman, G and Margolis, J (2012) Beyond Curriculum: The Exploring Computer Science Program, *ACM Inroads.* 3(2): 47–53.

Gove, M (2012) *Speech at the Bett Show Jan 2012.* Available at: **www.gov.uk/government/speeches/michael-gove-speech-at-the-bett-show-2012** (accessed 22 February 2017).

Grigg, R (2010) *Becoming an Outstanding Primary Teacher.* Harlow: Pearson Education.

Healey, M (2014) *Students as change agents in learning and teaching in higher education.* Available at: **www.mickhealey.co.uk/resources** (accessed 17 February 2017).

Hedderwick, M (1998) *Katie Morag Delivers the Mail*. London: Red Fox Books.

Helsper, EJ and Eynon, R (2010) Digital natives: where is the evidence? *British Educational Research Journal,* 36 (3): 503–520.

Herts for Learning (2016) *The Primary Computing Scheme V.5*. Available at: **www.thegrid.org. uk/learning/ict/foundation/** (accessed 17 February 2017).

Hewitt, K (2001) Blocks as a Tool for Learning: Historical and Contemporary Perspectives, *Young Children, January*, pp.6–13.

Hicks, D (2006) *Lessons for the Future: The Missing Dimension in Education*. Victoria BC: Trafford Publishing.

Hicks, D and Holden, D (1995) *Visions of the Future – Why we Need to Teach for Tomorrow*. Stoke on Trent: Trentham Books.

Huang Hsin-Yuan, W and Soman, D (2013) *A Practitioner's Guide to Gamification in Education*. Toronto: University of Toronto.

Huba, J and McConnell, B (2012) *Citizen Marketers*. Chicago: Kaplan Publishing.

Hughes, T (1968) *The Iron Man*. London: Faber and Faber.

IAB (2014) *Gaming Revolution*. IAB. Available at: **www.iabuk.net/research/library/gaming-revolution** (accessed 17 February 2017).

James, A, Smith, P and Radford, L (2014) Becoming grown-ups: a qualitative study of the experiences of peer mentors, *Pastoral Care in Education,* 32(2): 104–115.

Kapp, K (2012) *The gamification of learning and instruction: game-based methods and strategies for training and education*. San Francisco: Wiley.

Kazimoglu, C, Kiernan, M, Bacon, L and MacKinnin, L (2012) *Learning Programming at the Computational Thinking Level via Digital Game-Play*. International Conference on Computational Science, ICCS.

Kazu, IY, Kazu, H and Ozdemir, O (2005) The Effects of Mastery Learning Model on the Success of the Students Who Attended "Usage of Basic Information Technologies" Course, *Educational Technology and Society*, 8(4): 233–243.

Kerr, J (2015) *The Crocodile under the Bed*. London: Harper Collins.

Kipperman, D (2009) Teaching through technology concepts. Paper presented at the *Strengthening the Position of Technology Education in the Curriculum; PATT-22 Conference*. Delft, Netherlands, August 24–28

Lalley, J and Gentile, JR (2009) Classroom Assessment and Grading to Assure Mastery, *Theory into Practice*, 48(1): 28–35.

Leutenegger, S and Edgington, J (2007) *A games first approach to teaching introductory programming*. Proceedings of the 38th SIGCSE technical symposium on Computer science education, pp.115–118. New York.

Lewin, K (1951) *Field Theory in Social Science.* New York: Harper and Row.

Lin, J, Wang, P and Lin, I (2012) Pedagogy*technology: A two dimensional model for teachers' ICT integration. *British Journal of Educational Technology*, 43 (1): 97–108.

Livingstone, I and Hope, A (2011) *NESTA Next Gen: Transforming the UK into the world's leading talent hub for the video games and visual effects industries.* Available at: **https://www.nesta.org.uk/sites/default/files/next_gen_wv.pdf** (accessed 17 February 2017).

Lu, L and Ortlieb, E (2009) Teacher candidates as innovative change agents, *Current Issues in Education*, 11.

Ma, L, Ferguson, JD, Roper, M, Wood, M and Wilson, J (2004) *A collaborative approach to learning programming: A hybrid model.* Glasgow: The University of Strathclyde.

MacPhail, A and Tannehill, D (2012) Helping Pre-Service and Beginning Teachers Examine and Reframe Assumptions About Themselves as Teachers and Change Agents: "Who is Going to Listen to You Anyway?", *Quest*, 64: 299–312.

Marchel, C, Shields, C and Winter, L (2011) Preservice Teachers as Change Agents: Going the Extra Mile in Service-Learning Experiences, *Teaching Educational Psychology*, 7:2.

Markham, T (2016) *Ten Tips for Better PBL.* Available at: **http://pblglobal.com/blog/ten-tips-for-better-pbl/** (accessed 17 February 2017).

McGonigal, J (2011) *Reality is Broken. Why Games Make Us Better and How They Can Change the World.* London: Vintage Books.

Mercer, N, Dawes, L and Staarman, JK (2009) Dialogic teaching in the primary science classroom. *Language and Education,* 23(4), pp.353–369.

Microsoft (2016) *Kodu Game Lab.* Available at: **www.kodugamelab.com/** (accessed 17 February 2017).

Massachusetts Institute of Technology (MIT) (2015) *MIT App Inventor.* Available at: **http://appinventor.mit.edu/explore/** (accessed 17 February 2017).

Miller, C (2013) The Gamification of Education. *Developments in Business Simulation and Experiential Learning.* 40, pp.196–200.

MIT (2016a) *Scratch 2.0.* Available at: **https://scratch.mit.edu/** (accessed 17 February 2017).

MIT (2016b) *About Scratch.* Available at: **https://scratch.mit.edu/about/** (accessed 17 February 2017).

Mittermeir, RT (2013) Algorithms for Pre-schoolers - A Contradiction? *Creative Education*, 4(9): 557–562.

Morpurgo, M (2011) *Friend or Foe.* London: Egmont.

Morris, D and Burns, M (2013) Teaching and Learning with ICT: Overcoming the Challenges of Being a 21st Century Teacher, in Leask, M and Pachler, N (Eds.) *Learning to Teach ICT in the Secondary School.* (3rd ed.) Abingdon: Routledge.

Morris, D (2012) ICT and educational policy in the UK: are we on the way towards e-maturity or on the road to digital disaster? *Research in Teacher Education*. 2(2): 3–8.

Morschheuser, B, Werder, K, Hamari, J and Abe, J (2017) *How to gamify? A method for designing gamification*. Available at: **http://gamification-research.org/2016/09/how-to-gamify/** (Accessed 20th February 2017) etc.

National Association of Advisors for Computers in education (Naace) (2016) *Assessment*. Available at: **www.naace.co.uk/curriculum/assessment/** (accessed 17 February 2017).

Naace (2016) *Third millennium learning award - Gearies Infant School*. Available at: **http:// legacy.naace.co.uk/thirdmillenniumlearningaward/geariesinfantschool** (accessed 17 February 2017).

National Center for Women and Information Technology (2009) *Pair Programming in a Box: The Power of Collaborative Learning*. Colorado: s.n.

Ng, W (2012) Can we teach digital natives digital literacy? *Computers and Education*, 59 (3): 1065–1078.

Norman, D (2013) *The Design of Everyday Things*. New York: Basic Books.

O'Hara, D (2011) The impact of peer mentoring on pupils' emotional literacy competencies, *Educational Psychology in Practice*, 27(3): 271–291.

Office for Communications (2015a) *The UK is now a smartphone society*. Available at: **www. ofcom.org.uk/about-ofcom/latest/media/media-releases/2015/cmr-uk-2015** (accessed 17 February 2017).

Office for Communications (2015b) *Children and Parents: Media Use and Attitudes Report*, s.l.: OfCom.

Ofsted (2002) *Changing Schools: An evaluation of the effectiveness of transfer arrangements at age 11*. London: Ofsted HMI 550.

Ofsted (2009) *The importance of ICT: Information and communication technology in primary and secondary schools, 2005/2008*. London: Ofsted. Reference no: 070035.

Ofsted (2011) *ICT in Schools 2008–2011, an evaluation of information and communication technology education in schools in England 2008–11*. London: Ofsted. Reference no: 110134.

P21 (2016) *Framework for 21st Century Learning*. Available at: **www.p21.org/our-work/p21-framework** (accessed 17 February 2017).

Pachler, N, Preston, C, Cuthell, J, Allen, A and Pinheiro-Torres, C (2010) *ICT CPD landscape: Final report*. Coventry: Becta.

Palmer, S (2001) *How to Teach Writing Across the Curriculum at Key Stage 2*. London: David Fulton Ltd.

Papert, S (1980) *Mindstorms: Children, computers and powerful ideas*. New York: Basic Books.

Papert, S (1993) *Mindstorms* [2nd ed.]. New York: Basic Books.

Papert, S and Harel, I (1991) *Situating Constructionism.* Available at: **www.papert.org/articles/SituatingConstructionism.html** (accessed 17 February 2017).

Patterson, S (2016) *Programming in the primary grades: beyond the hour of code.* New York: Rowman and Littlefield.

Piaget, J (1955) *The Child's Construction of Reality.* London: Routledge and Kegan Paul.

Pound, L (2006) *How children learn.* London: MA Education.

Powell, R, Smith, R, Jones, R and Reakes, A (2006) *Transition from Primary to Secondary School: Current Arrangements and Good Practice in Wales.* NFER.

Prensky, M (2001) Digital Natives, Digital Immigrants, *On the Horizon,* 9(5).

Prestridge, S (2012) The beliefs behind the teacher that influences their ICT practices, *Computers and Education,* 58 (1): 449–458.

Price, J and Valli, L (2005) Preservice Teachers Becoming Agents of Change, *Journal of Teacher Education,* 56(1): 57–72.

Python Software Foundation (2016) *Python 3.0.* Available at: **https://www.python.org/** (accessed 17 February 2017).

Qualification and Curriculum Authority (QCA) (2007) *ICT Programme of Study and Attainment Target.* London: QCA.

Quince, A and Layman, M (2006) Pupil2Pupil Peer Mentoring, *Education Review,* 19(2): 85–89.

Resnick, M (2013a) *Learn to Code, Code to Learn.*
Available at: **www.edsurge.com/news/2013-05-08-learn-to-code-code-to-learn** (accessed 17 February 2017).

Resnick, M (2013b) Reviving Papert's Dream, *Educational Technology,* 52(4): 42–46.

Rising Stars (2016) *Switched on Computing.* London: Hodder Education.

Robbins, JN (2012) *Learning Web Design* (4th Ed) Canada: O'Reilly Media.

Robot Mesh (2016) *Flowol 4.* Available at: **www.flowol.com/Flowol4.aspx** (accessed 17 February 2017).

Rosen, M and Oxenbury, H (1993) *We're Going on a Bear Hunt.* London: Walker Books.

Royal Academy of Engineering (2014) *Applying Computing in D & T at KS2 and KS3.* London: s.n.

Royal Society (2012) *Shut down or restart? A way forward for computing in UK schools.* London: The Royal Society. Available at: **https://royalsociety.org/~/media/education/computing-in-schools/2012-01-12-computing-in-schools.pdf** (accessed 17 February 2017).

Ryan, R and Deci, E (2002) An Overview of Self-Determination Theory, in E Deci and R Ryan, *Handbook of Self-Determination Research.* Rochester NY: University of Rochester.

Sentance, S and Csizmadia, A (2015) *Teachers' perspectives on successful strategies for teaching Computing in school.* s.l., s.n.

Shin, N and Kim, S (2007) Learning about, from, and with robots: Students' perspectives. Paper presented at the *16th IEEE International Conference on Robot & Human Interactive Communication.* Jeju, Korea, August 26–29.

Siddiqui, N, Gorard, S and Beng, HS (2014) Is a Summer School Programme a Promising Intervention in Preparation for Transition from Primary to Secondary School? *International Education Studies*, 7(7): 125–135.

Sitthiworachart, J and Joy, M (2004) *Effective Peer Assessment for Learning Computer Programming.* Proceedings of the 9th annual SIGCSE conference on Innovation and technology in computer science education. pp.122–126. New York.

Slangen, L, Keulen, HV and Gravemeijer, K (2011) What pupils can learn from working with robotic direct manipulation environments, *International Journal of Technology and Design Education*, 21: 449–469.

Smith, GG and Grant, B (2000) From players to programmers: a computer game design class for middle-school children, *Journal of Educational Technology Systems,* 28(3): 263–275.

Softronics, Inc. (2016) *MSW Logo V.6.5b.* Available at: **www.softronix.com/logo.html** (accessed 17 February 2017).

Søndergaard, H and Mulder, RA (2012) Collaborative learning through formative peer review: pedagogy, programs and potential, *Computer Science Education*, 22(4): 343–367.

Stevenson, D (2008) *What is a "Change Agent"? Exploring the intersection of Computer Science and the Social Sciences.* Available at: **http://it.toolbox.com/blogs/original-thinking/what-is-a-change-agent-23764** (accessed 17 February 2017).

SurfScore Inc. (2016) *Kodable.* Available at: **www.kodable.com/** (accessed 17 February 2017).

Tennant, G and Harries, D (2012) Transition of Pupils from Key Stage 2 to 3, *Journal of the Association of Mathematics Teacher,* 226: 9–12.

Teo, T (2013) An initial development and validation of a Digital Natives Assessment Scale (DNAS), *Computers and Education*, 67: 51–57.

Time Magazine (1999) *People of the Century.* December 31, 1999, Vol. 154, No. 27

Toh, L, Causo, A, Tzuo, P, Chen, I and Yeo, S (2016) A Review on the Use of Robots in Education and Young Children, *Educational Technology and Society,* 19(2): 148–163.

TTS Group, Ltd. (2016) *Bee-bot App.* Available at: **www.tts-group.co.uk/tts-content/free-apps-for-our-floor-robots.html** (accessed 17 February 2017).

Vanderborght, B (2008) *Robots, binnenste buiten (Robots, inside out).* Sint-Niklaas: Uitgeverij Abimo.

Verlaan, B, t Veld, R, van der Veen, H, van Rij, V, Morin, P and Maassen van den Brink, H (Eds.) (2007) *Rapport horizonscan 2007, naar een toekomstgerichte beleids- en kennisagenda (report horizonscan 2007, to a forward-looking policy and knowledge agenda).* The Hague: Commissie van Overleg van sectorraden voor onderzoek en ontwikkeling, COS.

Vygotsky, LS (1978) *Mind in Society: The Development of Higher Psychological Processes.* Cambridge, MA: Harvard University Press.

Wang, Y, Ai, W, Liangi, Y and Liu, Y (2015) Toward Motivating Participants to Assess Peers' Work More Fairly: Taking Programing Language Learning as an Example, *Journal of Educational Computing Research,* 52(2): 180–198.

Wells, D (2012) Computing in schools: time to move beyond ICT? *Research in Teacher Education,* 2(1): 8–13.

Wiliam, D (2006) *Assessment for learning: why, what and how?* Available at: **www.dylanwiliam. org/Dylan_Wiliams_website/Papers.html** (accessed 21 February 2017).

Williams, LA and Kessler, RR (2000) All I really need to know about Pair Programming I Learned in Kindergarten, *Communication of the ACM,* 43(5): 108–114.

Williams, L, Layman, L and Hussein, K (2008) *Eleven Guidelines for Implementing Pair Programming in the Classroom.* Toronto: Agile Alliance.

Wing, JM (2006) Computational Thinking, *Communications of the Association for Computing Machinery (ACM),* 49(3): 33–35.

Wing, JM (2011) *Research Notebook: Computational Thinking - What and Why?' The Magazine of the Carnegie Mellon University School of Computer Science.* Available at: **www.cs.cmu.edu/link/ research-notebook-computational-thinking-what-and-why** (accessed 17 February 2017).

Wisse, M (2008) Robots, sensoren, algoritmes en motoren (robots, sensors, algorithms and engines). In Dijkgraaf, R, Fresco, L, Gualthe´rie van Weezel, T & van Calmthout, M (Eds.) *De be`tacanon, wat iedereen moet weten van de natuurwetenschappen (the science canon, what everyone should know about science)* (pp. 185–187). Amsterdam: De Volkskrant en Meulenhoff b.v.

Yaroslavski, D (2016) *Lightbot.* Available at: **http://lightbot.com/** (accessed 17 February 2017).

Index

Added to a page number 'f' denotes a figure and 't' denotes a table.
Page numbers in Roman numerals indicate glossary.